The Expansion Years

1857 to 1901

JAMES
BUCHANAN

ABRAHAM
LINCOLN

ANDREW
JOHNSON

ULYSSES S.
GRANT

RUTHERFORD
B. HAYES

JAMES A.
GARFIELD

CHESTER A.
ARTHUR

GROVER
CLEVELAND

BENJAMIN
HARRISON

WILLIAM
McKINLEY

by Rose Blue and Corinne J. Naden

RSVP
RAINTREE
STECK-VAUGHN
P U B L I S H E R S
The Steck-Vaughn Company

Austin, Texas

To the memory of Mary Lee Graeme and to Rose's mom,
two very gutsy ladies.

Published by Raintree Steck-Vaughn Publishers, an imprint of Steck-Vaughn Company

Publishing Director: Walter Kossmann   **Project Manager:** Lyda Guz
Editor: Shirley Shalit   **Electronic Production:** Scott Melcer
Consultant: Andrew Frank, University of Florida   **Photo Editor:** Margie Foster

Library of Congress Cataloging-in-Publication Data
Blue, Rose.
The expansion years 1857 to 1901 / by Rose Blue and Corinne J. Naden.
p.   cm. — (Who's that in the White House?)
Includes bibliographical references (p.   ) and index.
Summary: Describes the lives and political careers of the ten men, from James Buchanan to William McKinley, who served as president during the second half of the nineteenth century.
ISBN 0-8172-4302-X
1. Presidents — United States — Biography — Juvenile literature.   2. United States — Politics and government — 1857-1861 — Juvenile literature.   3. United States — Politics and government — 1861-1865 — Juvenile literature.   4. United States — Politics and government — 1865-1900 — Juvenile literature. [1. Presidents. 2. United States — Politics and government — 1857-1861 — Juvenile literature. 3. United States — Politics and government — 1861-1865 — Juvenile literature. 4. United States — Politics and government — 1865-1900 — Juvenile literature.]
I. Naden, Corinne J.   II. Title.   III. Series: Blue, Rose.   Who's that in the White House?
E176.1.B664   1998
973.8'092 — dc21   97-15038
[B]   CIP   AC

Acknowledgments
The authors wish to thank Harold C. Vaughan of Fort Lee, New Jersey, for his critical reading of the manuscript. Photography credits: Cover White House Photo; Title page (all) National Portrait Gallery, Smithsonian Institution; pp. 4, 6 The Granger Collection; p. 8 National Portrait Gallery, Smithsonian Institution; p. 11 North Wind Pictures Archive; p. 13 Library of Congress; p. 17 National Portrait Gallery, Smithsonian Institution; p. 18 The University of Michigan Museum of Art; p. 19 Corbis-Bettmann; p. 20 The Granger Collection; pp. 23, 25 Corbis-Bettmann; p. 29 The Granger Collection; p. 30 Culver Pictures; p. 31 National Portrait Gallery, Smithsonian Institution; p. 32 The Granger Collection; p. 34 North Wind Pictures Archive; p. 37 The Granger Collection; p. 38 Corbis-Bettmann; p. 39 National Portrait Gallery, Smithsonian Institution; p. 41 The Granger Collection; p. 42 North Wind Pictures Archive; p. 44 The Granger Collection; p. 46 North Wind Pictures Archive; p. 47 The Granger Collection; p. 48 National Portrait Gallery, Smithsonian Institution; p. 49 White House Historical Association; p. 50 The Granger Collection; p. 54 National Portrait Gallery, Smithsonian Institution; pp. 55, 56 The Granger Collection; pp. 59, 63 National Portrait Gallery, Smithsonian Institution; p. 66 North Wind Pictures Archive; p. 67 The Granger Collection; p. 69 (top) National Portrait Gallery, Smithsonian Institution, (bottom) North Wind Pictures Archive; pp. 70, 71, 73 The Granger Collection; p. 76 (top) National Portrait Gallery, Smithsonian Institution, (bottom) Corbis-Bettmann; p. 77 The Granger Collection; p. 79 National Portrait Gallery, Smithsonian Institution; p. 80 The Granger Collection; p. 82 Remington Art Museum, Ogdensburg, NY; p. 84 The Granger Collection.

Cartography: GeoSystems, Inc.

Printed and bound in the United States
1 2 3 4 5 6 7 8 9 0 LB 01 00 99 98 97

Contents

Increasing Prosperity and Gathering Clouds

*M*ost everything about the United States grew during the expansion years. Except perhaps the lives of its Presidents. From 1857 to 1901, ten men lived in the White House. Three of them were killed by assassins.

The expansion years may not have been healthy for Presidents, but it isn't surprising that there was lots of trouble. Rapid growth often turns the world upside down, for countries as well as for teenagers. And the country certainly was growing. When James Buchanan took office in 1857, the U.S. population was about 30 million. When William McKinley died in 1901, it was more than 76 million. In those 44 years called the era of expansion, the United States went from 32 states, when Minnesota entered the Union in 1858, to 44 states, when Wyoming entered in 1890. In addition, Secretary of State William H. Seward bought nearly 600,000 square miles of far northern land from Russia for $7.2 million. Most Americans thought that was an awful

The rush is on! Beginning on September 22, 1891, land-hungry homesteaders swarmed into present-day Oklahoma to stake claims to land taken from Native Americans.

lot of money for frozen snow, so they called the purchase Seward's Folly. That was back in 1867. Today, the area is still a lot of frozen snow, but it is also Alaska, the oil-rich forty-ninth and largest state.

The country was growing in other ways, too. Americans were making tracks for California at a furious rate ever since gold was discovered at Sutter's Mill in 1848. Hopefuls from the East poured into the West. The Union Pacific and Central Pacific linked up in Utah in 1869 and united the country by railroad. Andrew Carnegie started his steel empire in 1899. During the last years of the nineteenth century, thousands of immigrants came to America, mainly from Europe. Electricity was installed in the White House in 1891. The National League of Professional Baseball Clubs was formed in 1876. The Metropolitan Opera presented its first performance—*Faust*—in New York City in 1883. This was the heady, brash "gilded age." Most people wanted free public lands, no foreign competition, and the government to leave them alone!

But for all the growth and all the prosperity and all the change, everything was overshadowed during the expansion years by just one event: the Civil War. This terrible four-year-long fight set brother against brother, neighbor against neighbor, and state against state. In its own sad way, it nearly brought about another kind of growth. It came close to turning what was one country, the United States of America, into two.

The central cause of the American Civil War was slavery, especially its spread into the western territories. This was at the bottom of all disputes between North and South, but there were other disagreements as well. A long time before war, both sides argued over whether a state had the right to secede from the Union. The South said yes, the North said no. North and South disagreed over economics, tariffs, and a way of a life.

All this trouble had been brewing for a long time. Most Presidents did their best to avoid it. Then, Republican Abraham

In this lithograph Union troops (left background) charge Confederate soldiers during the Battle of Shiloh, April 6–7, 1862. The North suffered some 13,000 casualties, the South about 11,000 killed and wounded.

Lincoln, with his antislavery views and his strong belief in the Union, became the sixteenth President of the United States. This was the final blow for the South. It was time to leave.

So, South Carolina fired on Fort Sumter in 1861, and the bloodiest war in the history of the nation had begun. How bloody a war it was! More than 600,000 Americans lost their lives. When the war ended with a Northern victory, it did not bring real peace, not for a long time. Yet, it did change the country forever. So many had died. There was hardly a family that had not been touched in some way. Slavery was gone and with it the Old South. The door shut on the question of secession. It is not a word heard even in the angriest of state legislatures today.

A new kind of growth began. It was called Reconstruction. The South lay in shambles. Most of the major battles had been fought on its territory. Reconstruction was supposed to rebuild the South economically. It was also supposed to build some sort of racial equality and to punish those who were, in the eyes of Northern Republicans, traitors to the nation. But Reconstruction did not bring quite the hoped-for success. It did ease many problems for the ex-slaves and it did help to rebuild the war-torn region. It failed ultimately, however, because it could not force unwilling whites to cooperate with newly liberated blacks.

The ten men who lived in the White House during the expansion years were by and large not the most distinguished of leaders. Buchanan was often called indecisive. Johnson was nearly thrown out of office. Grant's administration was tainted by corruption. Hayes was sound of judgment and dull of personality.

Even so, things did happen and the country did change under these leaders. The policies that both Johnson and Grant pursued in Reconstruction changed life in the South, and even the North, forever. The Thirteenth, Fourteenth, and Fifteenth Amendments were revolutionary changes indeed. The Thirteenth Amendment, passed in 1865 under Johnson, abolished slavery. The Fourteenth Amendment, passed in 1869 under Johnson, established equal rights. The Fifteenth Amendment, passed in 1870 under Grant, gave the right to vote to all races regardless of skin color or past slavery. Women were not included in this new condition of fairness. They would not be granted this privilege until 1920.

Of all the Presidents in the expansion years, for all their shortcomings and their accomplishments, one stands out well above the rest. His name was Abraham Lincoln. His election and his presidency were crucial to the history of the United States. Because of who he was and where he was and what he did, he made a difference. Like George Washington, Abraham Lincoln came along at just the right time. Sometimes, even a country needs to be lucky.

Chapter One

Buchanan: Too Little, Too Late

James Buchanan (1857-1861)

*P*erhaps no President could have prevented the Civil War. Perhaps not the calm diplomacy of Washington, or the great intellect of John Quincy Adams, or even the blustery force of Andrew Jackson could have stopped those cannons from firing on Fort Sumter. Certainly James Buchanan could not. With two bitterly opposed sides threatening violence, Buchanan was sometimes indecisive, sometimes too concerned with remaining in the middle to be an effective leader. With the nation coming apart at the seams, it desperately needed a take-charge President. James Buchanan was not. He stood firmly on compromise. Earlier decisions, such as the Compromise of 1850 and the Missouri Compromise, had delayed major conflict, but they had not solved the basic issue. Relying on reason and high-mindedness, Buchanan could not bring himself to assert his authority when it was needed. What he did was too little—far too little and far too late.

To many, Buchanan's indecisiveness not only spelled disaster, but it was surprising as well. When he was elected in 1856, most people expected him to steer the troubled national ship right into clear waters. After all, he had been a capable public servant for 43 years. He was minister to Russia under Jackson and to England under Pierce. He was Polk's secretary of state and had served well and admirably. Now, here he was at age 65, a gentle, levelheaded, methodical man heading a quarrelsome country. Much was expected.

James Buchanan, six feet tall and heavy of build, was reportedly quite handsome. Even so, he was the nation's first and only bachelor President. Considering the spotlight on family life during presidential campaigns today, that record may hold for a while. He was engaged as a young man to Ann Coleman, but supposedly spent all his time at work. She broke the engagement, which was probably just as well since her family thought he was marrying her for her money anyway.

Actually, while still quite young, Buchanan amassed quite a fortune himself. He wasn't born wealthy, but he was a saver, kept accurate accounts of all his financial dealings, and knew exactly how much he spent to the penny. Perhaps he learned that from his storekeeper father, who emigrated from Ireland to settle near Mercersburg, Pennsylvania, where James was born on April 23, 1791. He was the second of ten children born to James and Elizabeth Speer Buchanan.

After graduating from Dickinson College in Carlisle, Pennsylvania, in 1809, Buchanan studied for the law. He was a state legislator by 1814 and a member of Congress by 1821. He backed Andrew Jackson for President, and Jackson made him minister to Russia in 1832. Two years later he was in the Senate, where he spent two terms. Buchanan was extremely careful in his Senate work, keeping accurate—to the smallest detail—accounts of everything. His colleagues admired his devotion to duty but generally fell asleep when he stood up in the Senate chambers. Buchanan was a most boring speaker.

Did this sort of plodding, if conscientious, service qualify a person to be President of the United States? It did in 1844. Buchanan's name was mentioned as a Democratic presidential nominee. But he lost out to James Knox Polk, who was elected and chose Buchanan as secretary of state.

Polk demanded that all his Cabinet members promise not to run for the presidency in 1848. By 1852, however, Buchanan had been bitten by the White House bug. This time he lost out to

Franklin Pierce, but was sent to England as the U.S. minister. Buchanan was lucky. He was gone during the congressional debate over whether to allow slavery in the Kansas and Nebraska territories. That meant he was not tainted by this bitter issue that divided the country.

When 1856 rolled around, the Democrats needed a candidate. About the only man they weren't mad at was Buchanan. In the race for the White House that November, he won against Republican John C. Fremont, but not everything was rosy. Although Buchanan had won in electoral votes, 174 to 114, he'd taken less than half the popular vote. Most of his strength had come from the South. His only Northern victories were Illinois, Indiana, New Jersey, and Pennsylvania.

Buchanan may have been a plodder, but he wasn't stupid. He knew he had to get back his Northern support. He would have to meet this slavery issue head on. For a time it actually looked as though he would. Instead, he edged the country one step closer to civil war.

First came the Dred Scott case and then the trouble over Kansas. Dred Scott was a slave, the property of a doctor in Missouri who took him out of the state on army assignments. In 1848, after the doctor's death, Scott sued for his freedom on the grounds that he had lived in Wisconsin territory, which was free. Scott lost the case in Missouri. But now he lived in another state, New York, and was able to take his case to the Supreme Court. The outcome didn't really matter to Scott himself because his new owner was antislavery and intended to free him anyway. However, the abolitionists, or those most strongly against slavery, were anxious to test this issue in court. Did or did not the Congress have the power to outlaw slavery in the territories?

Buchanan also wanted the Court to settle this question. On this issue, he was not at all indecisive. He knew exactly where he stood on slavery. He was for it. In his campaign he had said he was "not friendly to slavery in the abstract." What he meant was that he opposed it as an idea or a concept. But he also said that the rights of the South had to be protected just like any other part of the Union. That meant protecting slavery in the South.

Before Buchanan took office, he secretly urged one of the Supreme Court justices, Roger Taney, to make the decision on Dred Scott as broad as possible to settle this matter. Then, in his inauguration speech on March 4, 1857, Buchanan asked the American people to accept the Court's ruling "whatever it was." But Buchanan had already been told of the decision and had approved it. It was announced to the public two days later. The six-to-three Supreme Court ruling said that Dred Scott was a slave, not a citizen, and had no right to sue for anything. It also said that only a state, not a territory, could make a slavery decision. Scott was a slave in Missouri and would remain so.

The Dred Scott case of 1857 is one of the most important in American constitutional history. Not only did it stir up deeply rooted emotions in U.S. race relations, but it was a strong factor in hastening civil war.

If the President had hoped the Court's ruling would settle the slavery issue, he couldn't have been more wrong. The North was more furious than before. Now, all eyes turned toward Kansas.

This woodcut of Dred Scott was made in 1857.

The territory of Kansas was anticipating statehood in 1857. Buchanan appointed Robert J. Walker as the territorial governor. Walker quickly realized that most Kansans, by about four to one, were antislavery. However, the territorial government at the time was proslavery. Before Walker could get the statehood wheels rolling, territorial leaders met in the town of Lecompton and drafted a proslavery state constitution. It not only protected slavery, but it denied the voters a chance to vote on the issue at all. Consequently, when the constitution went for a vote, most Kansans stayed away from the polls.

Walker hurried off to Washington and asked Buchanan to reject the new constitution as being unfair and not representing the people. But the South had put Buchanan in office and he was much influenced by his southern-dominated Cabinet. He said no to Walker.

The President immediately ran up against powerful Senator Stephen A. Douglas from Illinois. Planning to run for the White House himself in 1860, Douglas knew he'd lose his home state if he approved the Lecompton constitution. Douglas told Buchanan he would have to go against him on this issue.

In the meantime, the voters in Kansas turned down the Lecompton constitution by 10,226 to 162. Now, Buchanan proved just how stubborn he could be. In early 1858, he still declared the Lecompton constitution to be legal and sent it to Congress for approval. A bitter debate raged. But with the help of Republicans and Democrats who backed Douglas, it was voted down. Kansas did not become a state—a free state at that—until 1861.

The fifteenth President of the United States had given the country a big shove toward war. There was no strong leadership when it was needed most. The South was enraged over the Kansas outcome but encouraged by Buchanan's attitude. The North was enraged by the South and disgusted with the President. It was a no-win situation. In addition, Buchanan's actions deeply split the Democrats. Once a national party, it was now divided into Southern Democrats who backed the President and Douglas Democrats of the North. The rift never healed. This had great consequences for the nation and, as it turned out, for the election of 1860.

Once a car gets out of control on an icy hill, it's sometimes impossible to stop. So it was with a nation sliding toward disaster. Buchanan was still involved with Kansas when he was hit with the Panic of 1857. This was an economic depression that badly hurt the industrial North and barely touched the

South, because demand for cotton remained high worldwide.

The rift between the two sections widened as Southerners began to feel slightly smug and Northerners slightly worried. Then, a new blow hit North-South relations. It was handed out by a white fanatic named John Brown. Violently antislavery, he had led a raiding party against slavers in Kansas in 1856 after claiming he was on a divine mission. Now he concocted a wild scheme to attack the federal arsenal at Harpers Ferry, Virginia. On the night of October 16, 1859, with 16

U.S. Marines storm the Engine House at Harpers Ferry to rout John Brown and his cohorts (based on a sketch made on the spot by a magazine artist).

whites and 5 slaves, Brown captured the arsenal. An alarmed President Buchanan sent Colonel Robert E. Lee and a small group of U.S. Marines to take it back, which they did. Ten of Brown's men died in the fight. He was wounded and captured.

Tried for murder and inciting slaves, Brown was convicted and then hanged on December 2, 1859. Frankly, almost all moderate Northerners condemned what Brown had done. However, at his trial, the excitable Brown suddenly turned calm and dignified. This was his last statement: "Now, if it is deemed necessary that I should forfeit my life for the furtherance of the ends of justice, and mingle my blood further with the blood of my children and with the blood of millions in this slave country whose rights are disregarded by wicked, cruel, and unjust enactments, I say, let it be done."

So, Brown was hanged and became an instant martyr in the North. This, of course, only angered the South more. The wedge was getting wider.

Although the growing sectional bitterness overshadowed everything else, Buchanan did have other victories while in office. He worked hard with Great Britain on how to interpret the Clayton-Bulwer Treaty, which had been signed in 1850. It was aimed at preventing both countries from interfering in South American politics. He also tried to get Mexico to allow American troops into its country if the government was threatened. He planned to enlarge the U.S. military as well and also to purchase Cuba, but the bickering Congress would have none of that.

The President also became involved in a strange war out West that is sometimes called "Buchanan's blunder." Brigham Young, head of the religion known as the Church of Jesus Christ of Latter-Day Saints, commonly called Mormons, was also the territorial governor of Utah in 1851. The following year, the Mormons largely ignored or openly defied the federal government, for instance, by approving polygamy, or multiple marriage. Buchanan replaced Young with Alfred Cumming and sent a 2,500-man army to restore law and order. The Mormons thought they were being invaded! A Mormon militia harassed government troops and murdered a number of non-Mormons on their way to settle in California. Finally, Buchanan sent a Mormon sympathizer to calm things down and Cumming was accepted as the new governor. That was also the end of Mormon direct political control over Utah territory.

Meanwhile, an ever more angry Congress blustered and threatened. Midterm elections had been bad for the Democrats, and now the presidential election neared. Curiously, Buchanan seemed above it all, saying "the prospects are daily brightening...the party will ere long be thoroughly united." If he was talking about his own party, it was a strange statement indeed. The President had already decided that he didn't want a second term. The Democrats were too split to rally behind anyone else. The South knew this and also knew that the new Republican party, favoring the North, was likely to get in. So it did in 1860, with the election of Abraham Lincoln.

Now the cries of secession began in earnest. They were loudest in South Carolina, which had long called for separation. Buchanan's response was to remain high-minded and appeal to reason. His reasoning urged everyone to wait and see what Lincoln would do once in office before taking any action.

The President may have thought his appeal sounded logical, but the South had other ideas. Between December 20, 1860, and the following February, with Lincoln not yet in office, seven states voted to secede from the United States of America in the following order: South Carolina, Mississippi, Florida, Alabama, Georgia, Louisiana, and Texas. By February 4, the Confederate States of America was formed, with the head of government at Montgomery, Alabama. Jefferson Davis of Mississippi was the president. The Confederacy would total 11 states when Arkansas, North Carolina, Tennessee, and Virginia seceded from the Union in April.

James Buchanan left office in March 1861. The government was in peril, the country even more so. The bright promise of a new land with freedom and justice for all was entering its darkest hour. The mess was now in Lincoln's hands.

Why had Buchanan failed? Surely the problems that led to the Civil War did not rest on his shoulders. But he did fail to step in quickly and strongly before South Carolina's threat became real. He tried to remain in the middle, soothing both sides but being firm with neither. Compromise had so often worked in this young land. Why not now? To be sure, Buchanan did not have Washington's diplomacy or Jackson's firmness. He also did not have congressional leaders who were willing to compromise. Instead of Daniel Webster or Henry Clay, now there was Jefferson Davis of Mississippi to champion the South or Charles Sumner, senator from Boston, whose great passion in life was the destruction of slavery.

Before Buchanan's death in 1868, he wrote that he could go to his grave with the "consciousness that I at least meant well for my country." So he undoubtedly did, this good man of conscientious ways and ideals of fair compromise. But he had not the temperament nor experience to put out the fires he had inherited. James Buchanan meant to do well. What he did was just too little, too late.

Names in the News in Buchanan's Time

John C. Breckinridge (1821–1875):

Buchanan's vice president from Kentucky. When Democrats nominated Stephen Douglas and Republicans named Abraham Lincoln for the election of 1860, Buchanan backed Breckinridge, choice of the Southern Democrats, in hopes of deadlocking the election and forcing Congress to select a moderate President. This naive plan backfired and Lincoln was elected.

Frederick Douglass (1817–1895):

African American writer, lecturer, son of a slave mother and a white father. Escaped from slavery (1838), settled in Massachusetts. Founded and edited the abolitionist newspaper, *North Star* (1847–1860). Helped recruit black regiments for the Civil War.

Harriet Beecher Stowe (1811–1896):

Connecticut-born author of *Uncle Tom's Cabin* (1851), whose publication inflamed antislavery sentiment in the North and is given much credit for hastening the Civil War. There is an old story that claims when Lincoln met her, he said, "So this is the little lady who started this big war."

Charles Sumner (1811–1874):

Four-term senator from Massachusetts, bitterly and violently antislavery. Urged immediate black suffrage after the war and took part in impeachment movement against Andrew Johnson. Sumner strongly denounced the Kansas-Nebraska Act in 1856, which compromised on the slavery issue by creating two territories and calling for the people to decide. Sumner labeled the authors of the act, Senators Andrew P. Butler and Stephen A. Douglas, proslavery. This so inflamed Butler's nephew, Preston S. Brooks of South Carolina, that he entered the Senate and beat Sumner severely with a cane. It took Sumner three years to recover.

Chapter Two

Lincoln: To the Ages

Abraham Lincoln (1861-1865)

What is there left to say about Abraham Lincoln? What hasn't been said or written about the sixteenth President of the United States? Everyone knows he was very tall and thin, sort of homely and serious looking, that he was born in a log cabin in the backwoods of Kentucky, that he had a quick, bright mind and pretty much educated himself. He is the last word on honesty, humility, and moral character. Abraham Lincoln is America's homespun hero. Well, not to everyone, of course. Prominent antislavery leader Wendel Phillips (1811–1884) didn't much like him. He called Lincoln a "first-rate second-rater." And Southern journalists didn't care for him at all. To them he was a "conniving emperor," a man who had "wrested freedom from the South on the pretense of saving freedom for the Union."

All that aside, whatever he was and wasn't, what Abraham Lincoln did do was rise "above politics into a timeless greatness" that no longer carries a partisan label. On anyone's shortest list of great Presidents, his name is bound to appear, usually first. As his sorrowing secretary of war, Edwin M. Stanton, said at Lincoln's death, "Now, he belongs to the ages."

Life for this homespun American hero began most simply in a one-room log cabin near Hodgenville, Kentucky, on February 12, 1809. In a few years, the family moved to Indiana. Lincoln's father,

This idealistic portrayal of Abraham Lincoln as a boy reading by the cabin fireplace was painted by Eastman Johnson in 1868.

Thomas, was a carpenter. Lincoln's mother, Nancy Hanks, died when the boy was nine years old. He later said, "I owe everything I am to her." His father remarried a year later, and young Abe loved his stepmother, too. Sarah Bush Johnston, a widow with three children, took loving care of Abe and his sister Sarah.

Lincoln grew up to be six foot four inches tall, muscular, good-natured, and somewhat moody. The Lincolns moved to Illinois in 1830. The following year, young Abe, now 21, struck out on his own. He worked on a Mississippi River flatboat delivering goods to New Orleans. In 1832, he spent a short time as a soldier. He volunteered to fight in the Native American uprising known as the Black Hawk War. Chief Black Hawk led his Sauk and Fox warriors in a brave attempt to regain land taken in the Midwest by the federal government.

Just as Lincoln had taught himself mathematics and grammar, so he taught himself law. He passed the bar examination in 1836 at the age of 27.

Lincoln moved to the new state capital of Springfield in 1837 and entered into a law partnership with John T. Stuart and later, with the well-known lawyer, Stephen T. Logan. In 1844, he joined William H. Herndon in a new law partnership. The two worked hard and were successful, but Lincoln began to think seriously about a life in politics.

Lincoln's first love affair ended sadly when Ann Rutledge died at the age of 19. Then, Lincoln met Mary Todd, who was visiting from Kentucky. They were married on November 4, 1842.

Mary Todd was 23, well educated, and quick tempered. Although the Lincolns loved each other, their marriage was often rocky and sometimes bitter. They had four sons, but only Robert, who was secretary of war under Presidents Garfield and Arthur, lived to adulthood. Edward died at age three, William at age 11 when the Lincolns were in the White House, and Thomas, called Tad because his father said he looked like a tadpole at birth, at age 18.

Always insecure and lonely, Mary Todd Lincoln suffered from increasing tantrums and painful scenes of jealousy. After her husband's shocking death, she traveled for some years, but became more and more depressed. Finally, she was declared insane and was committed to a private hospital in 1875. After her release the following year, she lived in France until shortly before her death in 1882.

Mary Todd Lincoln

From state government, Lincoln went on to Washington in 1847 for one term in Congress. A natural vote getter, he won election by the largest majority ever in his district. He was the only Whig elected from the state of Illinois. But after his term ended in 1849, Lincoln grew annoyed with politics and retired to his law practice for a few years. The old political fever returned, however, and in 1856 he joined the new antislavery Republican party. As he toured the state making speeches for presidential candidate John C. Fremont, Lincoln ran into Senator Stephen A. Douglas of Illinois. The two began to disagree out loud on the subject of slavery. Douglas defended the Supreme Court's decision on Dred Scott. Lincoln said that "any man who justifies the enslavement of others, justifies his own."

Exchanges of this kind got Lincoln's name in the news. He was nominated by the Republicans to challenge Douglas's Senate seat in 1858. When he accepted the nomination, Lincoln quoted from the Bible, saying, "A house divided against itself cannot stand." He also said words that he would later back up as President: "I believe this government cannot endure half slave and half free. I do not expect the Union to be dissolved..."

So began the famous 1858 Lincoln-Douglas debates. Douglas was a forceful, impassioned speaker, but homespun Abe proved his equal. Although they argued bitterly over the slavery issue, in reality they were not so far apart. Lincoln hated slavery, true, but he had fully as much horror of black and whites intermarrying as did Douglas. Yet, Lincoln truly believed the country could not endure half slave and half free, and on that basis alone, slavery must go.

In seven Illinois cities in 1858, Lincoln (at the podium, with Stephen Douglas standing behind him) debated the issue of permitting slavery in free territory.

Douglas regained his Senate seat. Lincoln said of his defeat that "It hurt too bad to laugh," but that he "was too big to cry." Adlai Stevenson used those same words when he lost the presidential election to Dwight Eisenhower a century later.

But that was the last election Lincoln lost. He was nominated for President on the third ballot of the Republican National Convention in May 1860. His running mate was Hannibal Hamlin of Maine, an ex-Democrat.

Considering that this election turned out to be certainly one of the most crucial in all U.S. history, it was preceded by a somewhat uninspiring campaign. The Republicans stood firmly behind Lincoln, who did not campaign actively. He stood on his previous comments about slavery and refused to say anything more on the subject. Actually, the Republican platform, consisting of its plans and principles, called for no slavery in the territories but no interference with already existing slave states. The Democrats were divided between North and South, with the Southern states warning that Lincoln's election would mean the end of states rights and, indeed, of freedom itself.

Lincoln was elected President of the United States on November 6, 1860. He carried all 18 free states and won 180 electoral votes out of 303.

Yet there was little time for joy. Convinced that the election of Abraham Lincoln would destroy the very foundations of the South, the state of South Carolina withdrew from the Union on December 20, 1860. When Lincoln gave his inauguration speech on the steps of the Capitol in Washington, D.C., on March 4, 1861, he faced a terrible reality. Between November and February, seven states had seceded from the Union and declared themselves a separate nation called the Confederate States of America, with Jefferson Davis as president. The nation was divided. At 4:30 A.M. on April 12, 1861, that division became the American Civil War. Confederate batteries opened fire on the federal garrison of Fort Sumter in Charleston harbor, South Carolina.

Twenty-three states of the Union, or the North, soon faced 11 states of the Confederacy, or the South. Arkansas, North Carolina, Tennessee, and Virginia had joined the original seven seceding states. On paper, the odds favored the North, which had a population of about 23 million. The South had only about nine million, including about four million slaves. However, the Confederacy had some strong points going for it. It seemed impossible that Northern ships could blockade the 3,500-mile-long Southern coastline. The South had a long, proud history of military tradition. The South expected aid from foreign countries (which it did not get). Southerners were fighting for that "intangible" called home and a way of life.

They also had Jefferson Davis, an extremely able Commander in Chief, firm, honest, and courageous, even though he was inclined to bristle at criticism. It wasn't so much that he failed, but that Lincoln didn't. To the surprise of many, Lincoln grew in stature and ability and ended up getting rather high marks for the way he waged the war.

However, what brought victory to the Union probably more than anything else was one great strength: its manufacturing. The North had some 100,000 industrial plants, the South about 18,000. The North was far superior in arms production. The North had 70 percent of all the country's railroads. It is said that an army marches on its stomach, but it also needs guns and ammunition and supplies and communication lines. Sometimes courage and honor just aren't enough. This time it took more than 600,000 deaths to prove it.

The Civil War was fought mainly on land, mostly Southern land. But naval power was important, too. The U.S. Navy didn't win the war so much as allow the land forces to win it. Here again, Northern industrial production was important. When the war began, the Union had 90 warships. When it ended, there were 626. The South had to start its navy from scratch and could never catch up.

Although most of the fighting was on land, there was a major naval battle at Hampton Roads, Virginia, on March 9, 1862. The North's *Monitor* met the South's *Virginia* (formerly the *Merrimack*). It was the first battle ever waged between ironclad ships. Although neither ship could sink the other, it showed that wooden battleships were now outmoded and it ushered in the modern navy.

The battle between the Monitor, *foreground, and the* Virginia, *lasted more than three hours. Neither ship was victorious.*

The world probably best remembers Abraham Lincoln during the Civil War for two documents that have become deeply etched in American history. One was the Emancipation Proclamation, the other the Gettysburg Address.

Although Lincoln truly believed in personal freedom, he had some worries about issuing the antislavery Emancipation Proclamation. He had pledged no interference with slavery in the states where it existed. He constantly said that his mission was to "save the Union...not either to save or to destroy slavery." He feared that any antislavery statement would force the slaveholding border states, Kentucky, Missouri, Maryland, and Delaware, to the Confederate side. Lincoln decided to wait for an important Northern victory before issuing his proclamation.

Then General George McClellan stopped General Robert E. Lee at Antietam in September. It wasn't the great decisive victory Lincoln had wanted, but it would have to do. The Emancipation Proclamation, which was officially signed on January 1, 1863, said that unless all rebel states returned to the Union by that date, all slaves in those states would be free.

Although the Emancipation Proclamation freed fewer than 200,000 slaves and applied only to those areas captured by the Confederacy, it had great symbolic value. However, it needed something else to make sure that this proclamation would have the force of law. That "something else" was

Lincoln visits General McClellan in his tent at Antietam. This photo was made by Mathew Brady, the famous Civil War photographer.

the Thirteenth Amendment, which outlaws slavery everywhere in the United States. It is part of Lincoln's greatness that he worked hard for passage of this amendment and made sure it was part of his party's platform when he ran for reelection in 1864. Unfortunately, he did not live to see the amendment ratified, which occurred on December 6, 1865.

The Gettysburg Address was delivered at the battle site in Gettysburg, Pennsylvania, on November 19, 1863. The President wasn't even the main attraction. Edward Everett of Massachusetts, the celebrated orator of the day, spoke for two hours. By that time, some of the crowd was bored and had wandered off around the battlefield. Lincoln spoke for three minutes. A photographer didn't even have time to get the camera ready before the President was finished.

Afterward, not a lot of people were impressed. Some journalists thought it was unworthy of the solemn occasion. Others found it "embarrassing" in its simplicity, proving once again that sometimes people who should know, don't. Actually, Lincoln didn't think much of it either. No one thought it would become an American classic.

Indeed, the Gettysburg Address has become one of the most quoted utterances of all time, a masterpiece of prose poetry. Its elegant phrasing begins:

> *Four score and seven years ago our fathers*
> *brought forth on this continent a new nation*
> *conceived in Liberty, and dedicated to the*
> *proposition that all men are created equal.*

It ends:

> *...that we here highly resolve that these dead*
> *shall not have died in vain—that this nation,*
> *under God, shall have a new birth of freedom—*
> *and that government of the people, by the people,*
> *for the people, shall not perish from the earth.*

Embarrassing simplicity indeed!

In the 1864 election, Lincoln, managing his own campaign, overwhelmingly beat Democrat George McClellan, 212 electoral votes to 21. He captured 55 percent of the vote, and nearly everyone in Union uniform voted for him. In fact, he gave furloughs to soldiers to help his reelection. Naturally, the 11 states of the Confederacy did not vote.

By early 1865, it was clear that Confederate forces were growing weak, although General Robert E. Lee courageously fought on. On April 9, 1865, at Appomattox Court House, Lee surrendered the tatters of his courageous Army of Northern Virginia to General Ulysses S. Grant. The elegance of Lee's surrender was matched by the fairness of Grant's terms.

The bloodiest, most horrific war ever fought on U.S. soil was over, although technically it did not end until the port of Galveston, Texas, yielded on June 2. It was won by Lincoln's statesmanship, by superiority of numbers, the increasing skill of military leaders, and mighty industrial resources. But the cost was staggering. The North suffered more than 350,000 dead and 275,000 wounded. There was scarcely a family in the South that did not lose a father, son, brother, or other relative. The South lost more than 250,000, with some 225,000 wounded. Nearly 185,000 African Americans—some 85 percent of those

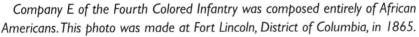

Company E of the Fourth Colored Infantry was composed entirely of African Americans. This photo was made at Fort Lincoln, District of Columbia, in 1865.

who were eligible—fought in the war. Not only did they fight bravely and face death in battle, but they faced death in capture as well. Many Southerners regarded black soldiers as runaway slaves, not prisoners of war, and either returned them to their former masters, or murdered them.

Economic losses were numbing. The war cost the United States about $15 billion! Even worse, the South was almost totally devastated. The wounds and the scars to people and country would take decades to heal. Some never have.

Most major battles during the Civil War occurred on the Confederacy's soil.

But the Union was preserved. Now what? Lincoln hadn't yet developed a clear plan for the war's aftermath. He wanted the Confederate states back in their "old position" in the Union. He didn't want so-called Carpetbaggers, Northern strangers, sent down to govern the South.

On Reconstruction, or rebuilding of the South, Lincoln was flexible. He appointed military governors to supervise the restoration. He promised to recognize any new state government that pledged loyalty to the Union and freed its slaves if it was backed by at least 10 percent of those who had voted in the 1860 election. That was not enough for many Northerners. They wanted retribution—make that revenge—not the same old Southern system!

For many in the North, however, Reconstruction was meant as a way to heal the nation, to make at least a step toward racial equality, and to help rebuild a devastated land. Some progress was made on all counts, but far less than at first anticipated. No amount of legislation could force a reluctant white population to cooperate with the former slaves.

So, President and Congress were in quarrelsome disagreement over the Reconstruction process. Then something happened to make the whole country forget Reconstruction for the moment.

On April 11, 1865, the Lincolns were entertaining in the Red Room of the White House. The President looked sad when he should have been happy. He recounted a recent nightmare in which he heard that the President of the United States was killed. By now the strain of the long and terrible war was evident. Indeed, pictures taken between 1861 and just before his death show the deep lines etched in his face and beneath his bushy eyebrows. Lincoln, incidentally, was the first President to wear a beard.

Like many a President past and present, Lincoln took an almost casual attitude toward the possibility of being killed in office. "If anyone is willing to give his life for mine," he said, "there is nothing that can prevent it." In fact, no one gave much thought to the possibility. It had never happened. All of the 12 Presidents deceased before 1865 died of natural causes. Fillmore, Pierce, and Buchanan were still living. In fact, it was not until after McKinley's assassination in 1901 that special guards, the Secret Service, were assigned to safeguard the President and his family.

There was no Secret Service in 1865, but the President did have four Washington, D.C., policemen assigned to him. They wore civilian clothes and carried .38 caliber revolvers.

On the evening of April 14, 1865, the Lincolns attended Ford's Theater in the nation's capital for a performance of the comedy *Our American Cousin*. During the third act, 26-year-old John Wilkes Booth, a member of America's most distinguished acting family of the nineteenth century, entered the President's box, found him unguarded, and shot him in the back of the head. Booth leaped to the stage, breaking a leg. Supposedly he shouted, "The South is avenged!" Some sources, however, say his words were, "Sic semper tyrannis," which is Virginia's state motto. The emotionally unstable Booth was a vigorous supporter of slavery and a hater of Lincoln. Twelve days later, a disfigured body was found in a burned barn in northern Virginia and identified as Booth.

The President was taken across the street to a boardinghouse. His tall body had to be laid diagonally across the bed. Lincoln was still breathing, barely, and five doctors worked over him all night long. But it was no use. Abraham Lincoln died at 7:22 the following morning, April 15. When young Tad Lincoln was told, he cried, "They killed my pa, they killed my pa."

The nation was stunned. Mary Lincoln slipped closer to madness. Over the next few days, thousands of Americans, black and white, walked solemnly past the President's coffin in the East Room of the White House. Said one, "Abraham Lincoln died for his country." Then began the 1,600-mile journey back to Illinois, stopping at many cities along the way so that his nation could

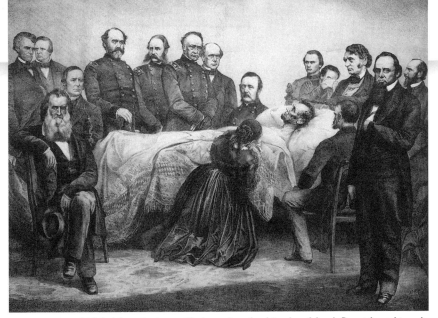

With his grieving wife kneeling by his deathbed, President Lincoln lingered until the next morning but never regained consciousness after the assassin's bullet entered his skull.

honor him. The man known as the Great Emancipator was buried on May 4, 1865, at Oak Ridge Cemetery in Springfield, Illinois.

Abraham Lincoln has become larger than life, sometimes seeming more myth than real. And although there may indeed be exaggerations of his life and deeds, his qualities of greatness were recognized even before his death. He was honest Abe, a man of courage, honor, insight, and resolution. He has been likened to George Washington, with good judgment, calm temper, and great firmness of purpose. That Lincoln loved his country, there can be no doubt. He was a self-made man who rose to greatness when nothing but greatness would do. Perhaps his secretary of war, Edwin M. Stanton, expressed the nation's feelings best of all when he said, "Now, he belongs to the ages."

Names in the News in Lincoln's Time

Jefferson Davis (1808–1889):

Born in Kentucky, West Point graduate (1828). U.S. senator from Mississippi, secretary of war to Franklin Pierce. Withdrew from Senate when Mississippi seceded. Elected president of the Confederacy (Feb. 18, 1861). Criticized for his hampering of field operations. Fled Richmond (April 1865), captured in May, indicted for treason (1866), released (1867). When others called for his death, Lincoln said, "Judge not, that ye not be judged." Retired to estate near Biloxi, Mississippi.

Stephen A. Douglas (1813–1861):

Born in Vermont, senator from Illinois. Known as the "Little Giant," challenged Lincoln in a series of debates for Senate seat, which Douglas won. His stand on slavery—"popular sovereignty"—helped drive a rift in the Democratic party. Died of typhoid fever at age 48.

Hannibal Hamlin (1809–1891):

Democratic turned Republican, senator from and governor of Maine. Lincoln's first vice president, became impatient with slow approach to emancipation; lost nomination for Lincoln's second term to Andrew Johnson. Minister to Spain (1881).

Jefferson Davis tries on a female undergarment in this contemporary cartoon of 1865. Davis was accused of trying to escape capture by Union soldiers by disguising himself as a woman. The story seems to have been a fabrication.

Chapter Three

Johnson and the Constitution on Trial

Andrew Johnson (1865-1869)

*P*oor Andrew Johnson. What a tough act to follow. Suddenly, on the morning of April 15, 1865, he was the head of a country whose citizens had stopped shooting at each other but hadn't shaken hands. A country filled with sorrow, lingering bitterness, and hatred. A country whose Southern lands lay in ruins. A country with thousands of newly free citizens without education, homes, or jobs. Add to that a country plunged into deep grief, including Johnson himself, over a martyred President whom a majority of citizens revered and adored.

It was not an ideal place to be. And although no one could loom larger than life after Lincoln, Johnson appeared pale and clumsy by comparison. In many ways, however, he should have been an ideal successor, if there was one. He was a Southerner but strongly pro-Union. He understood both those who would preserve the Union and those who would leave it. But he ran up against radicals in government over how the South should be reconstructed and by whom. Largely because he defied his own Republican party, Johnson became the first, and so far only, U.S. President to be impeached.

The word "impeachment" is usually used incorrectly when applied to government. It does not mean to remove from office. It means to indict, to bring charges against. According to the U.S. Constitution, only the House of Representatives has the power of impeachment. The Senate conducts the trial, which requires two-thirds of their number to convict, meaning in this case, removing a President from office. Such was the situation President Andrew Johnson faced on the afternoon of March 5, 1868, when the Senate proceedings began.

It was a long way from his humble beginnings. Humble, indeed, they were. Lincoln may have been born in a log cabin, but Johnson was born in a shack in Raleigh, North Carolina, on December 19, 1808. He was the second of two sons born to Jacob, a laborer who died when Andrew was three, and Mary McDonough Johnson. The boy never attended school and probably never saw a book until he began to work for a local tailor at age 15. There, he learned to sew and he taught himself to read.

Eliza McCardle Johnson

At age 18, Johnson moved to Greeneville in eastern Tennessee, where he opened a tailor shop and married Eliza McCardle. They eventually had four children. His wife was determined that he better himself and she helped to teach him to write. Johnson proved to be a good student. In 1834 he became mayor of the town and in 1835, a Tennessee state legislator. Initially, a Democrat, he entered the U.S. House of Representatives in 1843, became governor of Tennessee ten years later, and was elected to the U.S. Senate in 1857.

When the Civil War began, Johnson supported the Union even though his state seceded from it. After Tennessee fell to Union troops, Johnson was named its military governor in 1862. In spite of the fact that he was a Democrat, his Union loyalty brought its reward. He was put on the Republican ticket for Lincoln's second term. Lincoln believed that a so-called War Democrat would pull in more votes than a Republican, and he was right.

Andrew Johnson took the oath of office as vice president on March 4, 1865. He had been ill and was exhausted on Inauguration Day. Before his speech, he drank some brandy, which had an obvious effect on him. Actually a moderate drinker, Johnson sounded intoxicated during his speech and was forever dubbed a drunkard. That, however, proved to be the least of his troubles. A little more than a month later, after Lincoln's assassination, Andrew Johnson became the seventeenth President of the United States.

The new President faced a country that was emotionally upset and a White House that was physically upset. Exhibiting the worst in behavior, collectors had poured into the White House after Lincoln's death and took almost anything they could carry. By the time the Johnsons arrived, silverware was missing and parts of sofas and chairs had been cut out. Even some heavy furniture had been dragged away. During renovations, the Johnsons acted with calm and patience. When Mrs. Johnson, who suffered from lung disease, was ill, daughter Martha Johnson Patterson acted as official hostess. "We are plain people from the mountains of Tennessee," Martha said. "I trust too much will not be expected of us." In fact, a good deal was expected of them, and the Johnson White House responded with charm, good taste, and dignity that surprised and delighted Washington high society.

On the political side, it took about 30 days for the new President to realize he was between a rock and a hard place. He was a Democrat, even if not always a faithful party man. The government was in the control of Republicans. Some of them were so-called Radical Republicans. They wanted peace, to be sure, but a harsh peace. The former Confederacy must suffer. Take away their lands! Punish the sympathizers! Let voting laws limit the power of rebel leaders! At first, even the Radicals were pleased with Johnson. After all, he had long raged against rich slave owners. He had defended the Union. He seemed one of them.

How wrong they were! Johnson was still and always a Southerner. He believed in states' rights and had no interest in racial equality. Yet he intended to follow Lincoln's plans for Reconstruction. After all, he reasoned, why preserve the Union if, after the war, the victors prevent the Union from being reestablished?

Johnson quickly pushed ahead with his Reconstruction plans. The Republican-controlled Congress was outraged at the return to power of all the white aristocracy—in the form of new congressmen—that had led the South to war. It was also against the so-called Black Codes, regulations compiled in the Southern states to restrict the movement and labor of blacks. Congress promptly refused to seat the new Southern delegations.

By the midterm elections of 1866, everyone knew what the battle was. Congress felt it had the power, and therefore the right, to dictate government policy, and no system of checks and

As part of Reconstruction, the Freedmen's Bureau, a government agency formed in 1865 to help African Americans to adjust to freedom, established schools such as this one to assist in the education of the new citizens.

balances would stand in its way. The President saw himself as defending the Constitution and therefore the people.

The elections were close, but they went against the President. That was partly his own fault. He made a fool of himself and demeaned his office with taunting and intemperate remarks during his speeches, bringing on more cries—unproven—of heavy drinking. The Radicals won a majority and now Congress could override any of Johnson's vetoes.

That didn't stop a determined Johnson, of course. He promptly vetoed a civil rights bill in early 1867. Now things got really dirty. Congress passed three Reconstruction bills that Johnson believed to be unconstitutional. The first, passed over Johnson's veto, established martial law in the South. The second carried an addition that took away the President's role as Commander in Chief of the military. This Johnson signed because to do otherwise would have meant denying funds to the army. The third, passed over a veto, was the Tenure of Office Act. This took away the President's right to remove any federal official without consent of the Senate.

By this time the Congress was talking about impeachment. But on what grounds? Then Johnson himself came to the rescue and walked right into the trap nicely prepared by the Radicals. Defying the Tenure of Office Act, he asked for the resignation of his secretary of war (also Lincoln's), Edwin M. Stanton. Johnson believed Stanton to be on the side of the Radicals against him. Johnson was right. Stanton was on the other side, he refused to resign. Johnson fired him and appointed Ulysses S. Grant.

No one wanted to appear to be against Grant the war hero, so no one grumbled. But Grant himself had his eye on the White House for 1868, so when the Senate insisted that Stanton get his job back, Grant withdrew. The President then appointed Major General Lorenzo Thomas. Stanton refused to leave his office, and he swore out a warrant for Thomas's arrest. "Very well," said a determined Johnson, "that is the place I want it. In the courts."

On February 24, 1868, the Congress of the United States voted to impeach. The vote was 126 to 47. With much pomp and circumstance, the impeachment trial, presided over by Chief Justice Salmon P. Chase, lasted nearly three months. There were 11 counts of impeachment and lots of statements about having disgraced the Congress because he spoke "in a loud voice."

Actually, Johnson spoke in no voice at all because his advisers wouldn't let him attend the trial. Lots of people did though, and tickets were hard to come by. Johnson could hardly believe the whole procedure. "Impeach me for violating the Constitution!" he growled, the man who, according to his own lights, was devoted to protecting the Constitution.

The vote came on May 16, 1868. There were 54 senators at the time, with 36 needed to convict. The Senate chamber was packed and hushed. Finally, the voting came down to one man, freshman Senator Ross, a Radical from Kansas. He stood quietly, his face expressionless. "Not guilty," he said. The President and the Constitution had been saved. The embarrassing spectacle was over. Incidentally, so was Ross's career.

The Fourteenth Amendment became part of the Constitution on July 9, 1868. It provided for equal protection of the law to all citizens. The Fifteenth Amendment, passed in 1870 during Grant's administration, specifically prohibited states from denying rights on the basis of race.

Quite surprisingly, Andrew Johnson would have liked to have been nominated for a second term, if only to prove how right he was. But that was not to be. His party named Horatio Seymour, who lost to U.S. Grant later that year. By 1870, all the Southern states were back in the Union.

In his last message to Congress, December 1868, Johnson now warned that it was wrong to favor one race over another, be it white over black, or black over white. Unless cooperation between the two races was achieved, he said, there would be great hatred and unrest in the land. The ten-year period of

Reconstruction, no matter how well intended, did not solve the hatred or unrest. The new state governments of the South were generally governed by carpetbaggers (Northerners who had gone south), political groups of African Americans, and so-called scalawags (Southerners who collaborated with both groups). Southerners generally resented the new governments. Eventually, the South took back its governments and by the late 1870s, the Democrats were back in power in the Southern states.

Although memory of the administration of Andrew Johnson is forever bound to impeachment, it did have one very famous achievement. William H. Seward, Johnson's secretary of state, purchased Alaska from Russia in 1867 for $7.2 million. Although the deal was called Seward's Folly and "Johnson's polar bear garden," all in all, it turned out to be not a bad investment.

This 1872 caricature of a typical carpetbagger, a former Union general named Carl Schurz, is the work of famed political cartoonist Thomas Nast.

At the end of his stormy term, Johnson returned to Tennessee and ran for the Senate in 1875. When he won, he was nervous about actually taking his seat in Washington. He needn't have been. When he entered the Senate chamber, there was a round of applause and flowers on his desk. All the senators, including those who had voted to convict him, shook his hand. Unfortunately, Johnson's second Senate career was short. He died of a stroke on July 31, 1875, and is buried on a hilltop near Greeneville, Tennessee.

Andrew Johnson survived a time of turmoil, anger, indignity, and trouble. If nothing else, his term served an all-important purpose. He had assured the citizens of one obvious fact: the government of the United States of America would survive.

Names in the News in Johnson's Time

Salmon P. Chase (1808–1873):

New Hampshire-born, Dartmouth graduate, senator, Ohio governor, secretary of treasury under Lincoln; Supreme Court Chief Justice at Johnson's trial during which he worked to maintain a fair hearing.

William Henry Seward (1801–1872):

Skillful New York lawyer, governor, senator, masterful secretary of state under Lincoln and Johnson, purchased Alaska (1867).

Philip Henry Sheridan (1831-1888):

Entered army (1853). Rose to major general in Union forces during Civil War. Intersected Confederate Army retreat at Appomattox, forcing Lee to surrender to Grant (1865). Removed by Johnson as military governor of Texas and Lousiana (1867).

Edwin M. Stanton (1814–1869):

Brilliant Ohio lawyer, Lincoln's secretary of war who proclaimed him as belonging "to the ages"; joined Radicals and conspired against Johnson, who dismissed him, leading to impeachment.

Thaddeus Stevens (1792–1868):

Pennsylvania lawyer, dominant figure in the House of Representatives, waging relentless war against slavery. Led impeachment of Johnson and managed trial; died shortly after.

In this political cartoon of 1869, William H. Seward, Johnson's secretary of state (left), experiences the strong winds of the Reconstruction period, along with President Andrew Johnson (center), and Gideon Welles, secretary of the navy.

Chapter Four

Grant: Let Us Have Peace

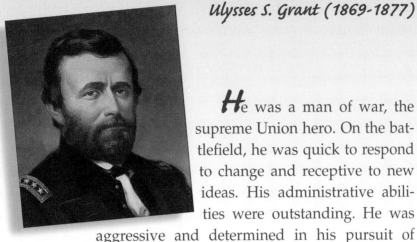

Ulysses S. Grant (1869-1877)

*H*e was a man of war, the supreme Union hero. On the battlefield, he was quick to respond to change and receptive to new ideas. His administrative abilities were outstanding. He was aggressive and determined in his pursuit of General Robert E. Lee and the Confederate armies. Yet, when the war ended, he was compassionate and respectful in the terms of surrender given to the great Southern leader. He said he never went into battle willingly. The sight of blood sickened him. After the Battle of Shiloh in 1862, he sat outside in the drenching rain so he would not have to watch his soldiers as the doctors attended them inside the hospital tent. His campaign slogan for the presidency in 1868 was "Let us have peace."

Ulysses S. Grant, the man of war, the man of peace, and the hero of the Union, did not have an easy time as President. At age 46, the youngest so far to take office, he was also the least experienced and probably had the least worldly wisdom. Nothing at West Point or on the battlefield prepared him to sit in the White House. He had only a limited understanding of economics and only a narrow view of the great power he now possessed. He saw Congress as making the laws and the President merely as executing them. He appointed government officials on the basis of loyalty, not competence. This, of course, had been done before and has been done since, but Grant brought it down to new levels. With the exception of able Secretary of State Hamilton Fish, Grant's Cabinet was a generally odd mixture. John Rawlins's only qualification to be secretary of war was that he was an old army buddy. The secretary of the navy, Adolph Borie, had one asset: he was rich. Grant's years in office were marked by corruption and scandal, as jobs were handed out to friends and relatives who had no other qualifications.

Grant was born in Point Pleasant, Ohio, on April 27, 1822, and remained nameless for a few weeks. His mother considered calling him Albert, then decided on Hiram and added Ulysses for the hero of Greek mythology. He later reversed his name to Ulysses Hiram, supposedly so that his initials would not spell HUG. However, it is hard to imagine anyone referring to him as HUG anyway. When he got to West Point, he was incorrectly registered as Ulysses Simpson (his mother's name) Grant, known to his classmates as "Sam" for U.S., or Uncle Sam. Throughout his lifetime, he signed his name as Ulysses S. Grant.

Grant's parents were Jesse, a leather tanner, and Hannah Simpson, who, her son later said, never cried. The boy's father had moved from Kentucky so as not to live where people owned slaves. Hiram Ulysses, the oldest of six children, spent his boyhood on a farm in Georgetown, Ohio, where the family moved in 1823. Although young Grant never liked farming, he did become skilled in handling horses. By the time he was 17, he had grown to only five feet one inch, but would grow another seven inches at West Point. He had small hands and feet, a pleasant, quiet manner, blue eyes, and red hair.

The teenager was not thrilled when his father got him an appointment to the U.S. Military Academy at West Point in 1839. He had no interest in the army. But he also realized that he had no other chance for more education. Although he called the academy "the most beautiful place I have ever seen," he was at best an indifferent scholar. His four years there were filled with demerits, and his only achievement seems to have been his horseback high jump record. It stood unbeaten for 25 years. Cadet Grant was sloppy, late for class, and unsoldierly. He graduated, somehow, in 1843, 21st out of a graduating class of 39 and 156th in conduct out of a total school enrollment of 223 cadets. In the mysterious ways of the military, his excellent horsemanship was recognized by not giving him duty in the cavalry. The new second lieutenant went to the infantry in St. Louis. His salary was $779 a year.

His new duty post, however, was fortunate in one way. Lieutenant Grant met the love of his life, Julia Dent, daughter of a well-to-do plantation owner and sister of a fellow cadet. Married on August 22, 1848, they enjoyed a happy and close 37-year union. The Grants had four children, and the whole family formed a merry group at the White House. In fact, Nellie, the youngest, was married there amid elaborate decorations in the great East Room. The only unhappy observer was said to be President Grant, who was losing his only, and adored, daughter to an Englishman, Algernon Charles Frederick Sartoris.

It was the Civil War that changed life drastically for U.S. Grant, as it did for so many other Americans of the time. In April 1861, President Lincoln issued a call for Union volunteers. Grant, who was strongly antislavery and very much opposed to secession, helped to train troops as a captain in

This photograph of Grant and his wife, seated in chairs, with other members of the immediate family, was taken in 1885 just prior to Grant's death.

Galena. In June, promoted to colonel, Grant headed the unruly 21st Illinois Volunteers and in August, a brigadier general, he was in command in southern Illinois and southeastern Missouri.

His military star then took a really fast track. He won the first major Union victory on February 16, 1862, on the Cumberland River in Tennessee, obtaining the surrender of 15,000 Confederate troops. As a major general, he drove back the Southern forces at Shiloh Church, April 6–7. Although the Confederates retreated, the heavy Union losses at Shiloh hurt Grant's reputation. However, he was a hero again after his victory at Vicksburg, on the Mississippi River, in July 1863. After the Battle of Chattanooga, in Tennessee, Lincoln named him commander of all Union armies. When Lee surrendered his tired forces at Appomattox Court House, Virginia, on April 9, 1865, it was to a saddened and equally tired General Grant, who was wearing a borrowed private's uniform—his was dirty—and muddy boots.

General Robert E. Lee of the Confederacy, seated at the table in Appomattox Court House, Virginia, signs the surrender papers as Grant, seated behind him to the right, looks on.

Grant's considerate attitude at the surrender earned him surprising honor, even in the South, which he toured after the war. In 1866, he was given the newly established rank of general of the armies of the United States. President Johnson, in a battle with Congress for government control, appointed him secretary of war. When Grant resigned at the insistence of Congress, which was out to prove its own power, Johnson's angry words strengthened Grant's ties to the Republicans. The popular war hero was nominated in 1868 with the slogan "Let us have peace."

Ulysses S. Grant was elected the eighteenth President of the United States in November 1868. He collected 214 electoral votes against 80 for the Democratic candidate Horatio Seymour, former governor of New York. Grant's running mate was Schuyler Colfax, congressman from Indiana.

Considering the scandals that wracked Grant's administration, it is somewhat surprising that he was the first President in 31 years to serve two full terms. Between Andrew Jackson, who left the White House in 1837, and Grant, ten Presidents were either not reelected, assassinated (Lincoln), or died in office during the first term.

Grant entered the White House at an exciting time, the so-called Gilded Age. A lot of people had made a lot of money during the war. It was an era of fabulous expansion, creativity, and energy. Growth was everywhere and displays of wealth became a passion. The larger, the gaudier, the better. Bribes were freely handed out, especially to politicians "for favors." What Americans needed from the White House was informed and decisive government. Unfortunately, they didn't get it from Grant. He seemed unwilling to consult with experts when problems arose. He was so in awe of the rich and influential that his judgment was often clouded when dealing with them. The Fisk-Gould scandal is a case in point.

Jim Fisk and Jay Gould were speculators in gold, and not honorable ones at that. They schemed to buy all the gold available in New York City, hold it for a price rise, and then dump it on the market to make tons of money. Of course, this plan wouldn't work unless the government withheld its own great gold reserves from the market. Fisk and Gould, who publicly entertained the naive President, tried—unbelievably!—to convince him of the soundness of their plan. In a rather vague way, the President seemed to agree. At least Fisk and Gould told speculators that he did. By September 24, 1869, the price of gold was so high that it affected many businesses. Panic flooded the market on "Black Friday." To get out of the mess he was partly responsible for creating, Grant ordered the Treasury to release federal gold. Gold prices fell and the market stabilized. Gould and Fisk were untouched, but many investors were ruined and the word "scandal" never quite left Grant's administration.

Despite the publicized corruption during Grant's first term, most Americans could not believe that their war hero was personally involved in the scandals. And so he easily won reelection in 1872 against Horace Greeley. Although Greeley campaigned for honest, clean government and was antislavery, he got only 66 electoral votes against Grant's 286. Newspaperman Greeley, who encouraged western development and said, "Go West, young man, and grow up with the country," died shortly after the election.

If Grant's first term was called corrupt, his second should have been labeled "you ain't seen nothing yet." In a masterpiece of understatement, Grant said at his second inaugural address that he had been the "subject of abuse and slander."

Perhaps the most famous—or infamous—scandal was the so-called Whiskey Ring. Whiskey distillers bribed government officials to save millions of tax dollars. Benjamin Bristow, who was Grant's secretary of the treasury, wanted to bring those involved to trial. One of them turned out to be the President's private secretary, General Orville E. Babcock. In a move that sent a strange signal regarding honesty, Grant defended Babcock and fired Bristow! After all, Babcock was an old friend!

In 1875, Thomas Nast drew this cartoon hailing Bristow's vigorous prosecution of members of the "Whisky Ring."

This was not an honorable time for the United States government. Washington was not, however, the only scene of corruption. Most of the nation's growing cities had problems, the most notorious being New York City and the Tweed Ring. Run by Democratic boss William Tweed, the party machine took bribes for favors and practically ran the government. It was broken up in 1871 when enough citizens and newspaper people got weary of it, and many members of the Tweed Ring went to jail.

Grant was discouraged—as well he might have been—at the end of his second administration. He said that his "failures have been errors of judgment, not of intent." That would seem to have been true. No one ever accused the President of personal corruption, but in hindsight he looks incredibly naive and insensitive. Perhaps someone should have told the old war hero that in the White House, unlike the battlefield, blind obedience rarely works.

Although scandal was the hot topic of Grant's years, he did approve amnesty—pardons—for Confederate leaders and he did support the civil rights of black Americans. He also had to deal with the Panic of 1873, a collapse in the nation's economy that followed the wild spending and growth era. Three years later, the nation grew physically with the addition of the 38th state, Colorado.

Strangely enough, the corruption of Grant's administration hardly lessened his popularity. He and his wife traveled to Europe, where they were generally received as royalty. When they returned during the Hayes administration, the scandals seemed to have been forgotten. His name was once again placed in nomination for the election of 1880. But the old war hero lost out to another survivor of the Battle of Shiloh, James Garfield.

No more politics said Grant. He and his wife moved to New York City, where they bought a mansion. When a brokerage firm in which he was a partner failed, Grant was penniless. Luckily for him, Congress restored him to full general's pay and rank.

Traffic was brisk around the White House by the time Grant left office in 1877.

But he needed more money. Author Mark Twain offered to publish Grant's memoirs.

The general accepted the offer, knowing he was dying of throat cancer. In increasing pain and losing the ability to talk or eat, Grant was determined to live up to his promise. The memoirs were finished on July 16, 1885, and they brought in $450,000 for his wife and family.

Besides the taint of corruption, Grant's administration was marked by the control of the so-called Radical Republicans. These leaders pledged to continue the harsh measures passed over the vetoes of President Johnson. Despite the fact that Grant professed to back Lincoln's moderate policies, Grant's administration saw the rise of vengeful government. Southern whites were angered and responded with vengeful and secret societies of their own. By 1870, the Ku Klux Klan had become a force in the South. It was bent on keeping African Americans from exercising their newly won rights. In 1871, Grant had signed the rather astonishing Ku Klux Klan Act, which allowed the federal government to interfere directly with the legal structure of the South. It was declared unconstitutional in 1882, but by that time, white Southerners were once again in control of the state governments.

Ulysses S. Grant died on July 22, 1885. His time in the White House may not have been distinguished, but his gallant service to his country during a terrible conflict was not forgotten. It is said that his funeral procession rivaled Lincoln's. Grant and his wife are buried in a tomb along Riverside Drive in New York City. The monument bears these four words: "Let us have peace."

Names in the News in Grant's Time

Schuyler Colfax (1823–1885):

Amiable vice president, Grant's first term. New York-born congressman from Indiana. Implicated in one of the worst scandals of Grant's presidency, he was, accused of accepting stock bribes. Allowed to finish his term but ruined politically and retired in 1873 in disrepute.

Hamilton Fish (1808–1893):

As secretary of state, he was the lone bright spot in Grant's Cabinet appointees. Born in New York, he was governor (1849–1850) and elected U.S. senator in 1851. Appointed secretary of state in 1869, he settled Civil War claims with Great Britain. Acted during Grant administration with honesty, common sense, and decorum.

Horace Greeley (1811–1872):

Born in New Hampshire, journalist, political leader; founded New York *Tribune*; antislavery. Badly beaten by Grant in 1872 election, died insane soon thereafter.

William Marcy Tweed (1823–1878):

New York City powerful political boss; dictated nominations for city mayor and state governor. Headed group known as Tweed Ring, which controlled city finances. Convicted in second trial after charges brought by *Harper's Weekly*, *New York Times*, and political cartoons of Thomas Nast (1870). Escaped to Spain, arrested, returned to New York City to die in jail.

"Boss" Tweed after his downfall in the New York City and state elections in 1871 was scoffed at by Thomas Nast in this cartoon.

Rutherford B. Hayes (1877-1881)

Rutherford Birchard Hayes was an old-fashioned man. He seemed old-fashioned even in the 1870s. Sickly and overprotected by his mother, he grew into a mild-tempered, fair-minded gentleman much given to high silk hats and black frock coats. His schedule varied little, even in the White House. He always took a nap after lunch.

If Rutherford B. Hayes were running for President today, he almost certainly would not be elected. He had absolutely no popular appeal, or what today we call "charisma." In fact, he has been called the most mediocre-looking man ever to run for President! He was short, and it is doubtful if his rat's nest beard ever felt a comb. During his campaign, the *New York Times* said he wore a "dreadfully shabby coat."

Even so, Hayes had some good things going for him. His integrity and good sense were unquestioned. He was without the slightest hint of corruption at a time when corruption seemed to run amok all around—and in—the White House. He tried very hard to bring stability to a country still reeling from Reconstruction. He was able and solid and reassuring—and old-fashioned. So, it seems strange that his should be the one presidential election whose results have been questioned. Did he deserve the victory?

Hayes was an Ohio boy, born in the town of Delaware on October 4, 1822. His father, Rutherford, a store owner, died before he was born. His mother, Sophia Birchard Hayes, overprotected this youngest and most frail of her four children. Young Rutherford attended Kenyon College and went on to Harvard Law School, graduating in 1845.

Hayes began to practice law in Lower Sandusky (Fremont), Ohio. In 1850, he started a practice in Cincinnati and gained a considerable reputation for his criminal cases. He also met Lucy Ware Webb and was smitten with her "beautiful dreamy eyes." Their most happy marriage began on December 30, 1852. Lucy Webb Hayes has the distinction of being the first First Lady with a college education, graduating from Wesleyan Female College in Cincinnati. Two customs began when she became First Lady. One survived, the other didn't. She started the practice of Easter-egg rolling on the White House lawn, which is still celebrated on the Monday following Easter Sunday. She also frowned on alcohol and wouldn't allow it in the White House, earning her the nickname of "Lemonade Lucy." Needless to say, that particular prohibition is long gone. Lucy Webb Hayes was also ardently anti-slavery and a champion of the poor. Rutherford and Lucy Hayes had seven sons and one daughter.

Lucy Webb Hayes

When the Civil War began in 1861, Hayes entered the army and rose to brigadier general in the Ohio Twenty-third Volunteers. He was wounded in action five times. He returned home to be elected to Congress and to the governorship of Ohio (1868–1872, 1876–1877). A reform governor, he called for worker safety codes and improved prison conditions. He supported the Fifteenth Amendment guaranteeing voting rights to all males.

In 1876, the Republicans were looking for a strong candidate who would make people forget the corruption in the last administration. They chose James G. Blaine of Maine, whose speaking elegance and congressional leadership earned him the title of the Plumed Knight. He got 285 votes on the first ballot. Hayes was on the candidate list, too, but he received only 61 votes, mostly from Ohio supporters. Sadly for Mr. Blaine, if not the country, rumors spread that he had used his office for personal gain. That was all the Republicans needed after the Grant scandals! Perhaps they had better nominate a Mr. Squeaky Clean—alias Rutherford B. Hayes—instead. He won on the seventh ballot. His running mate was a little-known New York banker, William A. Wheeler.

The Democrats also had reform and an end to scandal on their minds. They nominated Samuel J. Tilden of New York, who had helped to break up the notoriously corrupt Tweed Ring in New York City.

Actually, there wasn't a lot of difference between the two men or the two parties on issues during the election of 1876. So, Election Day 1876 came—and went. The 54-year-old Hayes was a saddened man that night, believing he had lost the election. According to reports, Tilden had taken the South as well as four Northern states and was 248,000 votes ahead in the popular count. More importantly, he needed just one more electoral vote to win. Hayes needed 20 to reach the necessary 185.

In this cartoon published in an American magazine just before the presidential election of 1876, Southern Democrats force black voters to vote for Tilden.

How could Tilden lose? But he did—by just one vote.

Returns were still out for the states of Florida, Louisiana, and South Carolina. If Hayes took all three, he would win with a total of 185, one more than Tilden. But was that possible, or even likely? In the strange world of politics, apparently so.

By the morning after with the election still in doubt, rumors began to spread, no doubt started by the Republicans. It was charged that African American voters in the three states in question were being harassed or stopped from voting by the Democrats. The result was chaos. Republican electors from the three states sent in their votes for Hayes. Not to be outdone, Democratic electors from the same three states sent in their votes for Tilden.

No one ever really knew the true vote in those Southern states. It does, however, seem somewhat likely that at least one of them would have gone for Tilden, thereby making him President.

But the reality was that Congress now had two sets of returns and no President. What to do?

The all-knowing U.S. Constitution had no answer to this problem, known as the Hayes-Tilden Affair. So, Congress appointed an electoral commission to decide the vote. It consisted of seven Republicans, seven Democrats, and one independent. The independent was David Davis, one of five Supreme Court justices on the commission. Just before the voting, Davis was elected to the U.S. Senate and had to resign from the Court. The justices, therefore, had to select another member to replace him. Republicans outnumbered Democrats on the Court. To no one's surprise, Davis was replaced with a Republican justice. Tilden was doomed.

The commission—no surprise again—voted a straight party line, eight to seven. Rutherford B. Hayes was elected the nineteenth President of the United States. But did he deserve the victory? Modern scholars generally think not, feeling that Tilden likely would have taken at least the state of Florida. But the deed was done, and Hayes is in the history books.

Why did the Democrats give in to this rather questionable election? In politics, the answer to such a question is usually a deal somewhere—not necessarily corrupt or even underhanded, but a deal nevertheless. In this case, among other things, the Democrats accepted the election of Hayes in return for control of the Southern states being given back to the South. Reconstruction, therefore, ended with Hayes and this compromise, and with it went many of the reforms that had sought equality among races. The African American was no longer a slave, but it may have seemed so. It would be a long time changing.

Although this cloud remained over his administration, Hayes tried to do his best. He supported fair treatment for all Americans and promoted a civil service system based on merit rather than influence. He said, "He serves his party best who serves his country best." He was determined not to be undermined by the scandals of the past. He appointed the most able men he could find for key positions. He declared that no one who worked for the federal government should take part in the management of political organizations or activities. In this, he won the battle but not the war. After requesting that two officials in the New York customhouse either quit their jobs or their political connections, he replaced them. One of the ousted was Chester A. Arthur, who became the twenty-first U.S. President. By his actions, Hayes ran into trouble with New York Senator Roscoe Conkling.

Like Presidents before and after him, the money issue plagued Hayes. The South and West wanted a return to silver coinage, outlawed in 1873. Hayes sided with the gold interests, backed by the East. Silver won, however, when the Bland-Allison Act of 1878, was passed over the President's veto. It required the U.S. Treasury to buy and coin two to four million dollars worth of silver every month.

While in office, President Hayes received an outstanding gift. Some years earlier, the British ship *Resolute* had become stuck in Arctic ice and was freed by a Yankee whaler. It was repaired in a U.S. port and returned to England. When the *Resolute* was dismantled in 1880, some of its oak timbers were made into a desk, which Queen Victoria presented to Hayes. Down through the years, many Presidents have sat behind that huge oaken desk in the Oval Office.

Hayes had long asserted that he would not seek a second term. He and his wife retired to Ohio, where he spent the next 12 years busying himself with his interests in education and prison reform. His beloved Lucy died in 1889, and the President four years later. A modest, able, dedicated leader, perhaps no one in the White House ever held a more profound sense of duty than Rutherford Birchard Hayes. How strange, then, that the question still remains—did this man deserve the victory that made him President?

Names in the News in Hayes's Time

Peter Cooper (1791–1883):

New York philanthropist, Greenback party candidate against Hayes in 1876, received only 1 percent of the vote. Founded Cooper Union for the Advancement of Science and Art (New York City), offering education to the poor.

William M. Evarts (1818–1901):

Boston-born chief counsel for Johnson at impeachment trial. Perhaps most able lawyer of his day. Led movement against corrupt Tweed Ring. Secretary of state under Hayes.

John Sherman (1823–1900):

Born in Ohio, most able financial expert and secretary of the treasury under Hayes; author of Sherman Anti-Trust Act (1890).

Samuel J. Tilden (1814–1886):

New York-born politician, led attack on Tweed Ring; Democratic candidate against Hayes; brilliant lawyer. Always maintained he was wrongfully denied the election of 1876. At death, bequeathed fortune to establish New York Public Library.

Chapter Six

Garfield: The Second Assassination

James A. Garfield (1881)

It wasn't healthy to be President of the United States in the second half of the nineteenth century. First, Lincoln, then Garfield; later, McKinley would be the third President in less than 40 years to die at the hands of a crazed person with a gun.

Ironically, President Garfield didn't really die from his gunshot wound. He more or less died from his doctors. They couldn't find the bullet and kept looking for about two months. The President kept getting weaker and weaker. The doctors poked and probed, spreading infection around his body because they didn't know enough about keeping their instruments sterile. All the time, the bullet was nicely lodged in his back muscles. It wouldn't have killed him. He should have been up and walking around, getting his strength back. But no one knew that in 1881. So President James A. Garfield spent just 199 days in office. His assassin was hanged.

James Abram Garfield was the third President (after Grant and Hayes) from Ohio, where he was born in Orange, on November 19, 1831. So far, seven U.S. Presidents have been born in Ohio, Harding being the last (1921–1923). Only Virginia, with eight, has more.

The youngest of five, James grew up in poverty on the family farm. His father, Abram, died when James was only two years old, and his mother, Eliza Ballou Garfield, worked hard to keep the farm and family together. When James had saved enough money he went to Massachusetts, where he graduated from Williams College in 1856.

Back in Ohio at the age of 24, his eastern education made him an important person. So much so that he was named the president of Hiram College in 1857. A year later, he married his childhood sweetheart, Lucretia Rudolph. Their happy marriage produced seven children, who would later bring a boisterous, lively atmosphere to the White House—an interesting change after the more sedate Lemonade Lucy.

In 1862, Garfield's home state sent him to the House of Representatives, where he would remain for 18 years. His keen mind and legislative skills were impressive, and he gained nationwide popularity over the years. But what he wanted was the Senate. At last, in 1880, his fellow Ohioans gave him that honor. Strangely enough, he never took his seat in the Senate.

That same year, the Republicans met in Chicago to decide on a presidential candidate. At the time, the party was divided. As often happens, when people are busy watching the front door, someone else walks

Lucretia Rudolph Garfield

in the back. U.S. Grant led all others for 33 ballots, but he could not get a majority. On the thirty-fourth ballot, Garfield's name was proposed. He objected—faintly. The deadlock was broken when Garfield was nominated on the thirty-sixth ballot. To calm the ruffled feathers of the Stalwarts, or conservative Republicans, the vice presidential candidate was Chester A. Arthur of New York. It was a move Garfield would not live to regret.

Facing another apparently squeaky clean nominee, the most damage the opposition could gather was that Garfield hadn't paid a tailor's bill when he was in New York. Forty-nine-year-old James A. Garfield was elected the twentieth President of the United States in 1880. His mother was the first ever to see her son take this oath of office. Garfield received 214 electoral votes to 155 for Winfield S. Hancock, the colorless Democratic candidate. The popular vote, however, was very close; only about 10,000 votes separated them.

The public got a different sort of President when Garfield took office. Tall, handsome, and gentlemanly, he was not only a teacher and a scholar, but a preacher as well. His elegant manner and soaring voice often held his audiences spellbound. Ulysses S. Grant wasn't so impressed, but that, of course, is understandable. Grant said of the new President, "Garfield has shown that he is not possessed of the backbone of an angleworm."

Whatever his backbone, the new President and his wife were warm, cultured people. This was, in general, a change for the White House, which had tended of late to house the more direct, homespun types that Americans often favored as their leaders. The President himself was a classical scholar, writing Latin and Greek. Lucretia Garfield began probably the first serious research on White House history.

There was little time for Garfield to prove his backbone or his ability since he was shot after only four months in office.

On the morning of July 2, 1881, Harry and James Garfield were in high spirits at the White House. They were about to take a train trip with their father. It was not to be.

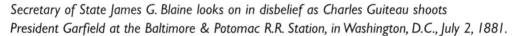

Secretary of State James G. Blaine looks on in disbelief as Charles Guiteau shoots President Garfield at the Baltimore & Potomac R.R. Station, in Washington, D.C., July 2, 1881.

As President Garfield entered the waiting room at the Washington train depot, an unhappy, out of work—and obviously deranged—office seeker named Charles J. Guiteau rushed at him from behind. He fired two bullets, one of them entering Garfield's back.

For two months the President lay in the White House growing weaker while his doctors tried to find the bullet. Frequent bulletins posted outside the White House gates kept the public informed of his weakening condition. The President once commented, "The people must be tired of hearing of my symptoms." He was wrong about that. Doctors even enlisted the aid of Alexander Graham Bell, who tried to find the bullet with his electrical listening device. Nothing worked. Lodged only a few inches from its entry point and relatively harmless to the President, the bullet eluded them.

The President's doctors weren't the only ones dealing with the shooting. Congress now had something new to worry about. For a short time after the shooting, Garfield had been unconscious. All during the 80-day period before he died, he was able to sign only one bill. Who is responsible for the country when the leader isn't? Should the vice president just act in the President's behalf or actually take over the office? The Constitution provided no clear answer, and this was one of the few situations that hadn't occurred to the Founding Fathers. It hadn't occurred to the Congress of 1881 either.

On September 2, the President's Cabinet held a meeting to discuss the problem. The Cabinet's decision was not to decide anything until Garfield could be consulted. But, of course, Garfield was in no condition to be consulted!

The ailing President asked to be taken to the seaside, where he hoped to gain strength. He did not. Too weakened to recover, Garfield died at Elberon, New Jersey, on September 19, 1881. Only once during his illness did Garfield mention his assassin. He said, "Why should he want to kill me?" Why, indeed.

And so, another presidential term was cut short. Charles J. Guiteau was convicted of murder and executed on June 30, 1882. With Garfield's death, Chester A. Arthur became the new President, which, of course, solved the problem of what to do when a President is ill—for the time being. If a problem was out of sight, it was out of mind for the Congress. It took 86 years for a reasonable solution to go into effect: The Twenty-Fifth Amendment to the U.S. Constitution was ratified on February 10, 1967. It said, among other things, that when the President gives Congress a written declaration of inability to discharge the duties of the office, the vice president becomes Acting President.

Names in the News in Garfield's Time

Alexander Graham Bell (1847–1922):

Born in Scotland; became a U.S. citizen in 1882. Patented telephone (1876); transmitted first wireless phone message (1880). Tried unsuccessfully to locate bullet that struck down Garfield (1881).

Samuel L. Clemens (1835–1910):

Celebrated American novelist, born in Missouri. Better known as Mark Twain. Among his most famous works:

The Adventures of Tom Sawyer (1876), *The Adventures of Huckleberry Finn* (1885), *A Connecticut Yankee in King Arthur's Court* (1889).

Henry Wadsworth Longfellow (1807–1882):

American poet, born in Maine. Famous works include: *The Village Blacksmith* (1841), *Evangeline* (1847), and *The Song of Hiawatha* (1855).

Victoria Woodhull (1838–1927):

Ohio-born reformer, first woman to run for U.S. President, by Equal Rights party (1872). Advocated equal rights for women and single standard of morality for both sexes.

Chapter Seven

The Cloudy Days of Elegant Arthur

Chester A. Arthur (1881-1885)

Whatever a U.S. President is popularly supposed to look like, Chester Alan Arthur surely fit the bill. A grand figure indeed was he: tall and sturdy, stately and handsome, with distinctive sideburns and mustache, natty attire, a fresh flower in his buttonhole, and a colored silk handkerchief showing from his pocket. The new President was a gentleman, educated, well read, and refined.

He was also a fusspot. Arthur was so appalled at the condition of the White House in 1881 that he refused to move in! "I will not live in a house like this," said he. And he didn't, not until some 24 wagonloads of mixed and battered furniture were sold at public auctions and the whole mansion was lavishly redecorated.

A recent and wealthy widower, Arthur had an extensive wardrobe that supposedly included 80 pairs of trousers! It is said he changed clothes for every occasion, often several times a day. No wonder he was known as Elegant Arthur!

Unfortunately for the President, his political life was not regarded as highly as was his social status. Linked to the fight between President Hayes and Senator Roscoe Conkling over collecting taxes for the port of New York, Arthur served his years in the White House under a cloud.

There is some dispute over the place of Arthur's birth. Most say Fairfield, Vermont, although some critics charged that he was actually born in Canada, which, of course, would have made him ineligible to be President. Such an accusation was never proven. The date of his birth was October 5, 1829. His minister father, William, was born in Northern Ireland, his mother, Malvina Stone, in Vermont. Chester was the fifth of nine children and was named for the doctor who delivered him.

The family moved to New York, and Arthur graduated with honors from Union College in Schenectady in 1848. He taught school for a time and studied law, earning his degree in New York City in 1854. As a lawyer, Arthur earned a fine reputation as a defender of the civil rights of African Americans.

In 1859, he married Ellen Lewis Herndon, who died at the age of 42 before her husband entered the White House. The Arthurs had three children.

During the Civil War, Arthur was put in charge of housing and equipping the thousands of soldiers pouring into New York City from all over the northeast. His efficiency, honesty, and integrity on the job drew him to the attention of Senator Roscoe Conkling, New York's Republican political boss and a favorite of President U.S. Grant. In 1871, Arthur was appointed customs collector for the port of New York City.

Ellen Herndon Arthur

The New York Customhouse had long been a notorious mess. Each time a new person entered the White House, hundreds of jobs changed at the Customhouse as political favors were paid and repaid. Arthur kept his integrity in this difficult position. Although he was never accused of being other than honest, he did continue to hire people in the same old way. If you were loyal to Senator Conkling, you had a job. That is, until Hayes succeeded Grant and decided to reform Civil Service. Arthur and another deputy, Alonzo Cornell, were then forced to step down.

When the Republicans nominated Garfield in 1876, Arthur was put on the ticket to appease the pro-Grant faction. To say

Chester Arthur was unqualified for vice president, much less President, is an understatement.

Arthur didn't help his own cause much either. Both before and after becoming vice president, he acted in a way that showed little knowledge of, or at least little respect for, his new position. During one speech, he seemed to imply that the whole Indiana election had been bought for the Republicans. When Garfield tried to weaken Conkling's power, Arthur openly took the senator's side against his own President. This certainly raised public eyebrows.

Then came the most unexpected. Garfield was assassinated. Chester A. Arthur, age 50, became the President of the United States on September 19, 1881. It is said that a friend's reaction was, "Chet Arthur, President of the United States! Good God!"

But, one never knows. All in all, Arthur performed rather better than expected in the White House. He walked a fine line between pressure from Senator Conkling and creating his own administration. He did replace six members of Garfield's Cabinet with his own selections, and they generally did their jobs well enough. He pressed on with the investigation of the Post Office frauds that had been opened during Garfield's short tenure, even though it caused embarrassment for his party. Twice he called on Congress for Civil Service reforms. The Pendleton Bill was signed in January 1883 and set up the Civil Service Commission to regulate conduct and qualifications for federal office. With his secretary of the navy, William E. Chandler, Arthur recommended rebuilding the U.S. Navy.

For the first three weeks of Arthur's presidency, there was no one to succeed him. If something had happened to him during that time, the nation would have been without a leader. There was no vice president, of course, and would be none until the next election. (The Twenty-Fifth Amendment of 1967 authorizes the President to nominate a vice president.) The next in line was the president pro tempore (for the time being) of the Senate;

today, it is the speaker of the House of Representatives. But the Senate had not elected a president pro tem at its last session. Until it did, there was no one next in line.

Arthur's push for government reform angered the conservatives in his own party who had always supported him. Without them, he lost the chance in 1884 to be nominated in his own right. The party picked James Blaine of Maine, but the Republicans would lose the White House anyway.

Elegant Arthur retired to New York, exhausted by the strain of office and an incurable kidney disease. He died less than two years later and is buried in Albany, New York. Historian Matthew Josephson said of Arthur that "he acted from the start with remarkable tact and grace." Mark Twain thought it "would be hard to better President Arthur's administration." Clergyman Henry Ward Beecher said, "I can hardly imagine how he could have done better." All in all, not faint praise for a man who spent his White House years under a cloud.

Names in the News in Arthur's Time

Susan B. Anthony (1820–1906):

Massachusetts-born organizer of the National Woman Suffrage Association (1869).

Clara Barton (1821–1912):

Founder of the American Red Cross and its first president (1882); born in Massachusetts.

Roscoe Conkling (1829–1888):

New York political boss; opposed Hayes and Garfield; mentor of Arthur.

Dorothea Dix (1802–1887):

Philanthropist and reformer, born in Maine. Superintendent of women nurses, Civil War. Sought reform in treatment for the insane.

Elizabeth Cady Stanton (1815–1902):

Women suffrage leader, born in New York. Organized first women's rights convention, Seneca Falls, New York (1848).

Grover Cleveland (1885-1889)

$\mathcal{G}$rover Cleveland was President twice. Not unusual, you say? In Cleveland's case, it was. Unlike all other U.S. Presidents who spent more than four years in the White House, Cleveland's second term did not follow the first. He was numbers 22 and 24 on the presidential list, with Benjamin Harrison in between.

Cleveland was unique in two other ways as well. A bachelor when elected, he was—and still is—the only President to be married in the White House. When President John Tyler married his second wife in 1844, the ceremony took place in New York City. But what surely made Grover Cleveland unique in all the history of politics was his advice to his aides during his first presidential campaign. When asked what they should say about a damaging accusation against him, Cleveland actually replied, "Tell the truth."

Stephen Grover Cleveland was born in Caldwell, New Jersey, on March 18, 1837. He apparently disliked his first name and stopped using it in his early twenties. He was the fifth of nine children born to Ann Neal and Richard Falley Cleveland, the local Presbyterian minister.

The family moved to central New York when Stephen Grover was four years old. Twelve years later, his hopes for a college education died along with the unexpected death of his father. He worked for a time in New York City, then ended up in

Buffalo, New York, where his mother's uncle, Lewis F. Allen, arranged for the young man to study law.

Cleveland passed the bar exam in 1859. He would spend many years in Buffalo, as assistant district attorney, sheriff, and finally mayor, on the Democratic ticket, in 1882. During the Civil War, Cleveland paid $150 for an immigrant to take his place in the army. This may not sound particularly patriotic, but it was a legal practice and not uncommon at the time. However, later on his political enemies used it against him.

Cleveland's efficient administration as mayor prompted the *Buffalo Sunday Times* to suggest him for state governor. He was overwhelmingly elected in 1883 and set out to prove his slogan that "Public office is a public trust." He insisted that federal jobs be given on merit, not favor and signed a state civil service bill into law. It had been sponsored by a new and brash young assemblyman named Theodore Roosevelt.

By the time the Democrats met in Chicago to nominate a candidate for the 1884 election, Cleveland clearly was a favorite. Not of everyone, however. His opposition to the corrupt bosses of Tammany Hall, New York's political power group, threatened his nomination. But the rest of the convention loved him, and the 46-year-old Cleveland was nominated on the second ballot, with Governor Thomas A. Hendricks of Indiana as his running mate.

The Republicans named James G. Blaine of Maine, who had come close to being nominated twice before, in 1876 and 1880. What a mudslinger this campaign turned out to be! The two men might as well have run for dogcatcher as far as issues were concerned. Everything was about personal morality! Blaine, while in Congress, had apparently profited from some shady railroad stock interests. The so-called Mugwumps, including Theodore Roosevelt, had fled the Democratic party and refused to support Blaine. Their title came from an Algonquin word meaning "big chief." It soon came to mean any independent voter. Now, the Mugwumps found and published a note Blaine had written about his stock deal. He had ended the note with "Burn this letter!" This gave the Democrats their campaign song: "Blaine, Blaine, James G. Blaine, The continental liar from the State of Maine, Burn this letter!"

The Republicans were having fun, too. They uncovered the charge of a young widow living in Buffalo that the unmarried Cleveland was the father of her son. He neither denied nor confirmed the charge, but agreed to accept responsibility and pay for support of the child. The Republicans sang, "Ma! Ma! Where's my pa? Gone to the White House. Ha! Ha! Ha!"

This might have been Cleveland's downfall except that he responded by instructing his aides to "tell the truth." This was so astonishing in bigtime politics that it clouded the issue. The child spent some time in an orphanage, was adopted by a well-to-do New York family, and eventually became a doctor.

With the aid of the Mugwumps, Cleveland won a narrow victory, 219 electoral votes to 182 and a margin of only one percent in the popular vote. Blaine did not help his cause any by being a fantastically dull-witted campaigner. He was present at a speech given by New York ministers in which one of his supporters said that the Democrats were a party of "rum, Romanism and rebellion." Perhaps Blaine was just too tired to catch this slur on the Catholic religion. He ignored it, and that promptly lost him most of the Catholic vote. In another foolish move, while the country was suffering through high unemployment, Blaine was seen dining in style with business tycoons John Jacob Astor and Jay Gould. That cost him the labor vote.

Grover Cleveland stepped into the White House on March 4, 1885. He would be the only Democratic President between 1861 and 1913! Even without the White House spotlight, it would have been hard to miss him. By this time, he had grown into a huge man, 5 feet 11 inches and 250 pounds. Except for William Howard Taft—who weighed in at 340 pounds!—Cleveland was our heftiest President. He had huge hands, a double chin, and a thick neck. His thinning hair was offset by a great bushy mustache. He loved to drink beer, smoke cigars, and fish, and his energy was inexhaustible.

He was sometimes known as antisocial, quick-tempered, blustery, and a generally irritable chap. But Washington society noted that his personality took a decided change for the better after June 2, 1886. The 49-year-old President married 21-year-old Frances Folsom of Buffalo, a graduate of Wells College. Cleveland worked that day until the ceremony in the Blue Room, with music provided by John Philip Sousa. The bride's train was 15 feet long, and the word "obey" was left out of the ceremony.

Grover Cleveland's marriage to Frances Folsom in June 1886 has been the only marriage of a President in the White House to date.

This youngest First Lady ever brightened Washington society as well as her husband's life. They would have five children. Some years after Cleveland's death, she remarried, becoming the first First Lady to do so. In 1947, she was buried in Princeton, New Jersey, next to the President.

The new President was bent on keeping his image of honesty. He vetoed hundreds of private pension bills as being a drain on the economy. He signed the Dawes Severalty Act, granting full citizenship to Native Americans and returning some lands taken from their reservations. He tried to reform the practice of awarding jobs for political favors. This was difficult and not always successful. Cleveland said that the stream of people who wanted favors from him "makes me feel like resigning."

Cleveland also had to deal with labor problems. Labor unions were growing in size and strength during the 1880s, pushing—

against obvious management opposition—for an eight-hour workday. But the labor unions received a serious setback in May 1886. A bomb was thrown at Chicago policemen who were trying to break up a workers' meeting in Haymarket Square, Chicago. Seven policeman and two workers died, and many more were wounded. Many people thought the United States was in danger of revolution. The Haymarket riot gave the U.S. labor movement a severe defeat.

Another big issue during this time was the question of lowering the tariff. Cleveland fought for it, claiming a high tariff hurt farmers and laborers. This annoyed big business interests. Cleveland's tariff stand cost him several key states in the election of 1888 and probably the presidency. Republican Benjamin Harrison beat him, 223 electoral votes to 168.

Cleveland dusted off his law degree and, with his family, moved to New York City. He had actually accomplished little during his administration, although he had certainly grown in leadership skills. However, he seemed to enjoy his return to private life and spent several vacations on Cape Cod, Massachussetts. About his only step back into politics during

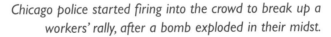

Chicago police started firing into the crowd to break up a workers' rally, after a bomb exploded in their midst.

this period came in 1891 when he wrote his famous "silver letter" to congressional Democrats. In it, Cleveland said he opposed the free coinage of silver and called it a "dangerous and reckless experiment." Fellow Democrats were not pleased. At this time, the Populist movement was gaining power. Pledged to the reform of agriculture, the Populists, among other things, wanted unlimited coinage of silver, aimed at putting farmers on a par with business and industry. The Populists put up candidate James B. Weaver in the 1892 election. He lost but made a good showing. Although the movement would collapse by the end of the decade, it was a challenging protest.

After his defeat in the election of 1888, it looked as though the political career of Grover Cleveland was over. Actually, he did not even seem to care. But, once again, in politics, one never knows...and four years can be a long, long time.

Names in the News in Cleveland's Time

James G. Blaine (1830–1893):

Senator from Maine; unsuccessful presidential candidate (1876, 1880); loser in 1884 election to Cleveland principally for not responding to "rum, Romanism and rebellion" speech.

Andrew Carnegie (1835–1919):

U.S. industrialist, born in Scotland. Entered steel business (1865), founded Carnegie Steel (1899), merged into U.S. Steel (1901). Retired, devoted life to distributing large fortune.

Thomas A. Edison (1847–1931):

Ohio-born inventor, established workshops in Menlo Park and West Orange, New Jersey; amassed more than 1,000 patents, including electric light; produced talking motion pictures (1913).

John D. Rockefeller (1839–1937):

New York-born oil magnate. Organized Standard Oil; established four great charitable organizations, including Rockefeller Foundation.

Chapter Nine

Harrison: Wrong Place, Wrong Time

Benjamin Harrison (1889-1893)

*I*f there is such a thing as an inherited gene for the White House, Benjamin Harrison surely had it. His great-grandfather, Benjamin, signed the Declaration of Independence. His grandfather, William Henry, was the ninth President of the United States (1841). This grandfather-grandson was one of three sets of Presidents with the same name. John and John Quincy Adams were father and son, and Theodore and Franklin Roosevelt were fifth cousins.

Harrison was a rather strange-looking man. He was about five feet six inches tall and stocky. His large paunchy torso sat on short stubby legs. Blue-eyed and red-bearded, he was the last U.S. President to wear a full beard. The fact that he was known as the "human iceberg" says a good deal about his personality.

Even though he lost the popular vote by 90,000, Benjamin Harrison won more electoral college votes and was inaugurated in March 1889. He stands, bareheaded in the rain, with his hand on the Bible.

Benjamin Harrison hated small talk. When you sit in the White House, that can be a problem. Except for his wife and two children, whom he adored, he was stiff and formal with most people. A dignified and colorless figure, he was without the "common touch," much less that twentieth-century necessity—charisma.

What Benjamin Harrison did have, however, was intelligence, honesty, integrity, and devotion to duty. Too bad, indeed, that those qualities were not enough to make him more effective.

Expansion fever was still gripping the country. During Harrison's term, North Dakota, South Dakota, Montana, Washington, Idaho, and Wyoming joined the Union, for a total of 44 states. Some historians have called this time the "period of no decision." America was rushing headlong from an agricultural economy to an industrial one. With this expansion came enormous problems in the cities and on the farms. Farmers feared that their way of life was fast disappearing. And it was! The railroads had opened the country from coast to coast. Businesses prospered and farm prices fell. Farmers grew ever more discontent. But there was trouble in the exploding cities too. Expansion meant problems with the labor force. Streams of immigrants were pouring into America. This constant wave of new people

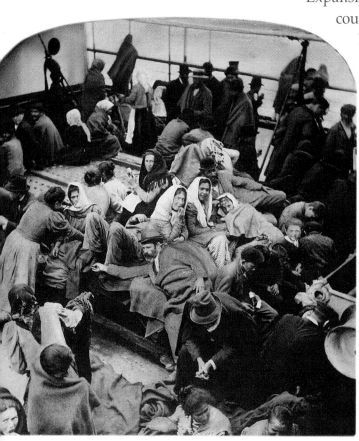

Immigrants, such as these on the deck of a ship arriving in New York from Europe, came by the thousands at the turn of the century, swelling the population figures.

created gigantic labor unrest and great fear among American citizens. They saw their jobs and their security disappearing with a labor market that would work for lower wages. Through all this, the American public generally felt that the nation's leaders were not paying attention to their plight. Government and the people were poles apart. What did it matter who sat in the White House or the halls of Congress, the people thought. Who paid attention to their unrest? Who was listening?

President Harrison and other leaders certainly knew what was happening. Yet, they seemed not to understand how the people felt about all these rapid changes. And so the gulf widened between the people and their leaders. The coldly honest, dignified, formal Benjamin Harrison was not the man to build a bridge.

Harrison was the fourth of seven Presidents from Ohio. He was born on August 20, 1833, in North Bend, Ohio, to John and Elizabeth Irwin Harrison. His father was a farmer and congressman, the only man to be the son of one President and the father of another.

Benjamin was seven years old when his grandfather, William Henry Harrison, became President and nearly 17 years old when his mother died. He graduated from Miami University of Ohio in 1852, near the top of his class. After wrestling with thoughts of becoming a minister, he decided on the law and passed the bar in 1854.

By this time, Harrison had married another Miami student, Caroline Scott, and they moved to Indianapolis, Indiana. There he formed a law partnership with William Wallace and won the race for city attorney in 1857.

During the Civil War, Harrison became a colonel in charge of the 70th Regiment of Indiana Volunteers. He left the army as a brigadier general.

Caroline Scott Harrison

Harrison was elected to the Senate in 1881, but was out again in 1886 when the Democrats, with Cleveland in power, gained control of Indiana.

Two years later, the Republicans decided that President Grover Cleveland, with his unpopular stand on the tariff, could be beaten. Harrison gave a speech in Chicago in which he recalled his Civil War duty. He was a fine speaker and brought back all the war-hero emotion of earlier years. But compared to the past, the election campaign of 1888 nearly put voters to sleep. Where was all that mudslinging! The only issue was the tariff. Harrison supported high tariffs; Cleveland supported low tariffs. Cleveland made just one public appearance the entire time. Harrison spoke only from his home in Indianapolis. The result was close, but no White House for Cleveland.

With Levi P. Morton as his running mate, Benjamin Harrison, 55 years old, became the twenty-third President of the United States. He lost the popular vote but beat out Cleveland in the electoral college, 233 to 168.

The Harrisons moved into the White House, where the First Lady put up the first Christmas tree, in 1889. But first she asked for money from Congress to do something about the rodent population that was sharing their home. With that taken care of, new plumbing and bathrooms were added, and in 1891, electricity! The problem, however, was that Caroline Harrison was afraid of this new invention and refused to turn off the switches. If no one was around, she had to retire with all the lights on until someone came by to turn them off!

The new President didn't have much time for electric light switches. He had hardly opened and closed the White House door before he was in trouble. During his campaign speeches from home, he had stressed that his administration would carry out major civil service reform—that old theme. But once in office, he was practically powerless to do so. The Republicans simply owed too many favors not to pay somebody back. In this

Joseph Keppler drew this "Bosses of the Senate" cartoon in 1889 attacking
the giant corporations and their control of members of the Senate.

way, for instance, department store owner John Wanamaker, who had been responsible for millions of dollars in campaign money, became postmaster general.

In 1890, the Republicans put three laws through Congress that tried to protect domestic industry and curb abuses. They did little or else just turned voters away. The Sherman Anti-Trust Act made it unlawful to take part in a contract or trust that would be in restraint of trade. Corporations formed "trusts" that controlled market prices and killed competition. This especially affected farmers and small businesses. But since the Sherman Act failed to make clear what "trust" or "restraint" meant, it was hard to understand. The Sherman Silver Purchase Act was passed to soothe western silver and farm interests. It said that the Treasury had to buy a certain amount of silver at market price each month. Many who bought the silver notes immediately redeemed them for gold, seriously depleting the nation's gold reserves. The law was repealed in 1893. The McKinley Tariff Act was supposed to protect domestic industry from imported products, but it so increased consumer prices that people reacted by voting for the Democrats.

Harrison was not winning any popularity contests at home. Surprisingly enough, however, he was quite diplomatic in two foreign affairs. He calmed an irate Italian government after three of its citizens were arrested in New Orleans on murder charges. And he threatened war against Chile after an incident involving the death of American sailors. Chile settled the incident peacefully

Election time rolled around again. Cleveland was back on the Democratic ticket and it looked like steady Harrison would be back in the White House. But things had changed in four years.

Once more, another unexciting campaign. But the results were different in 1892. Cleveland was in, Harrison was out. He lost by an electoral count of 277 to 145.

Back home in Indianapolis, the former President practiced law once more. His wife had died in 1892, just two weeks before Election Day, causing both candidates to stop campaigning. Four years later, the 62-year-old Harrison married a 37-year-old widow, Mary Dimmick.

In 1901, Harrison caught the flu, which developed into pneumonia. He died on March 16 and is buried in Indianapolis. His second wife survived him by nearly half a century.

Lots of people had differing opinions of Benjamin Harrison. Theodore Roosevelt didn't seem to like him much. Observed the future President in 1890: "He is a cold-blooded, narrow-minded, prejudiced, obstinate, timid old psalm-singing Indianapolis politician." Speak your mind, Mr. Roosevelt!

Still, Harrison was not without those who praised him. According to poet James Whitcomb Riley, "A fearless man inwardly commands respect, and above everything else Harrison was fearless and just."

He seems to have been all those things—just and true and sincere, perhaps a little cold-blooded and narrow-minded, too. He does not rank high on the list of effective and outstanding Presidents. Unable to communicate well with the people he governed, Harrison turned out to be the wrong man at the wrong place in the wrong time.

Names in the News in Harrison's Time

Samuel Gompers (1850–1924):

English-born labor leader. Organized Cigarmakers' Union (1877); president American Federation of Labor (1886–1924).

Liliuokalani (1838–1917):

Queen of the Hawaiian Islands, succeeded her brother, King Kalakaua, on throne (1891); overthrown (1893) supposedly with backing of American interests.

Levi P. Morton (1824–1902):

Vermont-born American banker; U.S. minister to France (1881–1885); Harrison's vice president (1889–1893); governor of New York (1895–1897).

Booker T. Washington (1856–1915):

African American educator, born a slave in Virginia. Established and headed Tuskegee Institute (1881) in Alabama. Gained national recognition. Author of *Up From Slavery* (1901).

Grover Cleveland (1893-1897)

"**W**elcome back, Mr. President! How does the White House look to you after a four-year absence?"

"Pretty much the same, I would say. Of course, things will be a little different this time."

"How so, sir?"

"I take it you haven't seen Ruth."

Grover Cleveland was back in the White House in 1893, now the twenty-fourth President of the United States. The vice president this time was Adlai E. Stevenson of Illinois. Cleveland's hair was a little thinner perhaps and his weight still pushed 250. However, a big change had occurred in the White House in the person of 17-month-old Ruth. The Clevelands' little daughter soon became the delight of all visitors. There were lots of those. At the time, it was not uncommon for perfect strangers to "drop in" to look around. Ruth was such a popular attraction and so many people picked her up that one morning no one could find her!

Grover Cleveland and his family relax on the steps of their home in Princeton, New Jersey, in 1907, after his two terms as President.

76

She was located unharmed, but that did it for Mrs. Cleveland! No more visitors streaming in. The Clevelands had two other daughters during the President's second term and two sons after that. Esther, born in 1893, was the first, and so far only, child of a President to be born in the White House.

What is generally said to be Cleveland's "finest hour" as President occurred early in his second term. The failure of the Philadelphia and Reading Railroad touched off the Panic of 1893. This was the most severe economic depression the country had yet experienced. It lasted four years. Cleveland placed the blame on the Sherman Silver Purchase Act, passed under the previous administration. He urged its repeal to stop the drain on gold reserves. A divided Congress argued for several weeks and came up with a compromise plan. The President got so angry, he supposedly banged his fist on the table and refused to budge from his stand. Congress repealed the Sherman Act in October 1893.

With continuing economic problems, strikes and riots broke out across the country. The worst was the Pullman strike of 1894. Strikers under the leadership of Eugene V. Debs walked out and crippled railway traffic from Chicago to the West Coast.

Cleveland's response was to send 2,500 federal troops to Illinois against the governor's wishes. Cleveland said the strike interrupted passage of U.S. mail. The strike was broken and Debs was arrested.

Business leaders and people in general praised the President,

During the Pullman strike of 1894, Chicago police used nightsticks to beat back a mob of rioting workers to allow a train to pass.

but gone was any support he had from labor. Cleveland was generally praised, however, in foreign affairs for his handling of the dispute over Venezuela's boundary. Great Britain had been arguing for some time about the border between Venezuela and the royal colony of British Guiana. Cleveland brought up the handy Monroe Doctrine. It reminded the English to stay out of affairs of the Americas. Cleveland did push for arbitration, however, and the matter was settled in 1899, in Britain's favor.

Grover Cleveland left office for the second time in 1897.

The United States had now grown to 45 states, with the addition of Utah the year before. Because of his stand on gold and his problems with labor, Cleveland was not a popular man. He died of heart failure on June 24, 1908. His last words were "I have tried so hard to do right." He is buried in Princeton.

Cleveland was quickly forgotten by his party once he left office. But in the following years, his reputation was revived. Today, historians generally place him somewhere in the list of "near greats." He is also remembered as that rarity in political circles who once said, "Tell the truth."

Names in the News in Cleveland's Time

Eugene V. Debs (1855–1926):

Socialist presidential candidate born in Indiana. Became national secretary of Brotherhood of Locomotive Firemen (1880); led Pullman strike in Chicago (1894), ended by Cleveland. Arrested and sentenced to six months' imprisonment for contempt of court. Sentenced to ten years for violating Espionage Act; released 1921.

Adlai E. Stevenson (1835–1914):

Vice president, Cleveland's second term. Born in Kentucky, congressman from Illinois. Grandfather of namesake who unsuccessfully opposed Dwight D. Eisenhower in 1952, 1956 elections.

Chapter Eleven

McKinley: Let the Good Times Roll!

William McKinley (1897-1901)

*T*he organizers of the Pan American Exposition in Buffalo, New York, were pleased to have the twenty-fifth President of the United States in their midst. On September 6, 1901, William McKinley stood in a receiving line to shake the hand of everyday citizens. When he faced Leon F. Czolgosz, an unemployed millworker from Detroit, he might have noticed that the man's right hand was bandaged. The bandage concealed a .32 revolver. Czolgosz fired two bullets point-blank at McKinley. One entered his stomach. McKinley fell back into the arms of a guard. After two operations, the President died on September 14.

Czolgosz was tried and convicted. He died in the electric chair in New York on October 29, 1901. "I killed the President," he said, "because he was the enemy of the people—the good working people. I am not sorry for my crime."

Lots of other Americans were, however. They stood silently as the President's funeral procession rode by in Canton, Ohio, where he is buried. With McKinley also died an era—the end of the era of expansion, the beginning of the progressive years. He was the last occupant of the White House to serve in the Civil War and the first since then to preside over a war of his own. He was a friendly, cheerful man, a brawny figure at five feet seven and almost 200 pounds. Always neatly dressed, he usually wore a white vest and a red carnation. He was also the only President between Andrew Johnson and Woodrow Wilson without a beard or mustache! His country was changing from a mainly agricultural society to a giant of industry, with all its fantastic growth and huge problems. And yet William McKinley seemed of another era, a time of courtesy and quiet enjoyments, without vanity or affectation. A time that would not come again.

McKinley was another Ohio boy, the fifth of seven Presidents from that state. He was born in the country town of Niles on January 29, 1843, the seventh of nine children born to William and Nancy Allison McKinley. After private school near Youngstown, he entered Allegheny College at age 17. But first ill health and then lack of money forced him to withdraw. When the Civil War broke out, he joined the Union Army. As an

Ida Saxton McKinley

infantry lad, his commander called him "one of the bravest and finest." His commander was another Ohioan and another President, Rutherford B. Hayes.

Back home, young McKinley studied law and passed the bar in 1867. He practiced in the city of Canton, where he met attractive Ida Saxton. They were married in early 1871 and had two daughters, both of whom died when very young.

McKinley was elected to the Senate in 1877 and served for 14 years. In 1890, he made a national name for himself with the McKinley Tariff Act, which raised duties on many imports up to the highest levels at that time. Shortly before, McKinley had met Marcus A. Hanna, an Ohio industrialist. With Hanna's support and aid, McKinley was elected governor of Ohio and served two terms (1892–1896).

With his experience as governor and the backing of Hanna, William McKinley was the Republican nominee for President in 1896. His Democratic opponent was William Jennings Bryan of Nebraska.

It was a strange campaign. Bryan was just 36 years old and a masterful orator. To deliver his stirring messages, he traveled all over the country in just three months—without an airplane! But he had very little money to back him. McKinley, however, had tons of money from Hanna and didn't go anywhere! He sort of campaigned from his front porch in Canton. Hanna-sponsored delegations trooped into Canton by train almost daily. On one day alone, McKinley spoke to about 30,000 people from his front porch! Small wonder he won the election, 271 electoral votes to 176. His vice president was New Jersey's Garret A. Hobart.

Once in office, the 54-year-old President's first act didn't surprise anyone. He restored the Republican tariff. Cleveland had replaced the McKinley Tariff Act with the Wilson-Gorman Act. Now McKinley replaced that with the Dingley Bill, raising protective tariffs to the highest rates ever.

All domestic issues, however, were soon overshadowed. The United States became preoccupied with a new war. In his inaugural address, McKinley had said that he wanted "no wars of conquest." But many Americans now called for this one, known as the Spanish-American War of 1898.

For some time, American sympathies had been with the people of Cuba, who were struggling for independence from Spain. Reports of Spanish atrocities, true enough but often exaggerated in the press, whipped up more sentiment. McKinley hoped to find a peaceful answer through diplomatic channels.

But that was impossible after February 15, 1898. The U.S. battleship *Maine*, on a courtesy call to Cuba, blew up and sank in the Havana harbor. Some 260 of the crew died. Today, many experts believe that the explosion was accidental, caused by some problem within the ship itself. But at the time, the American public blamed Spain. Inflamed by the William Randolph Hearst newspapers, the cry went up of "Remember the *Maine*!"

The *Maine* incident gave McKinley little choice. He told Spain that the United States demanded peace, which meant, of course, that the island of Cuba must be freed. Although the Spanish knew they had lost Cuba, they would not also lose face by surrendering without a fight. So began the Spanish-American War.

It was declared on April 25, 1898. It ended with the Paris Peace Treaty, ratified on February 6, 1899. The short conflict gave the United States the chance to show off its modernized navy, which had been steadily improving for the past 15 years. When war was declared, Commodore George Dewey had a fleet of six ships in the Pacific. On May 1, he sent most of Spain's Pacific fleet to the bottom of Manila Bay in the Philippines. Dewey did not lose a man. The country was ecstatic!

Meanwhile, U.S. troops, including Theodore Roosevelt and his First U.S. Volunteer Cavalry, popularly known as the Rough Riders, were scoring victories in Cuba. A cease-fire was declared on August 12, 1898. Fewer than 400 Americans were killed in action. Thousands though died from yellow fever and malaria. Two years later, Dr. Walter Reed would prove that the deadly yellow fever was transmitted by the mosquito.

Teddy Roosevelt and the Rough Riders, mostly on foot because their horses were left behind in Florida, charge up a Cuban hill. It was probably Kettle Hill although later accredited as San Juan Hill even by Roosevelt himself.

The Spanish-American War freed Cuba from Spain, although it remained under U.S. protection until 1934. The war also brought Puerto Rico, Guam, and the Philippines into the sphere of U.S. territories and established the United States of America as a world imperial power. Philippine independence was granted in 1946. Puerto Rico is still a self-governing commonwealth of the United States, and Guam is a self-governing U.S. territory.

McKinley's next foreign problem concerned China. The President had authorized Secretary of State John Hay to institute the China Open Door policy. The United States urged all major powers to follow the practice of allowing equal opportunity for all participating nations to trade freely with colonies or developing countries. This applied particularly to the right to trade with China. There was great competition among the Western powers for exclusive trading rights with China.

But in 1900, a group of Chinese nationalists, in an action known as the Boxer Rebellion, killed hundreds of foreigners and terrorized others in Peking (now Beijing). The nationalists were known as Boxers because of the rituals they performed with their fists as they got ready for battle. McKinley sent 5,000 U.S. soldiers to help protect the foriegn legations in the city.

Prosperity had returned, Americans were feeling good, and McKinley was voted back in the White House in 1900. Although he declared he'd "had enough of the job," he ran anyway. Hobart having died in office, Theodore Roosevelt was his running mate this time. This was an interesting choice since two years earlier when he was secretary of the navy, Roosevelt had said that the President "has about as much backbone as a chocolate eclair." Presumably people look different when one is vice president. The Republicans picked up 292 electoral votes against 155 for William Jennings Bryan and the Democrats.

As prosperity continued into his second term, so did McKinley's popularity. The good times were rolling. Unfortunately for the President, the good times lasted only six more

months until he was shot by the anarchist Leon Czolgosz in Buffalo, New York, on September 6, 1901, and died on September 14 (see page 79). McKinley thus became the third President of the United States to die at the hands of a disgruntled citizen with a gun.

Leon Czolgosz shoots President McKinley at close range during the Pan-American Exposition in Buffalo, New York, September 6, 1901.

Names in the News in McKinley's Time

George Dewey (1837–1917):

Annapolis graduate from Vermont; destroyed Spanish fleet in Manila Bay (1898). Admiral U.S. Navy (1899).

Marcus A. Hanna (1837–1904):

Wealthy businessman and influential adviser to McKinley. U.S. senator from Ohio (1897–1904).

William Randolph Hearst (1863–1951):

Head of newspaper empire. His papers were often called examples of "yellow journalism," included *San Francisco Examiner*, *Chicago American*, *New York Journal and Mirror*. Born in San Francisco, he was influential in inciting anti-Spanish feelings over Cuba.

Garret A. Hobart (1844–1899):

New Jersey-born lawyer, banker, U.S. vice president, McKinley's first term. Ability and prestige so great that newspapers referred to him as the "assistant president."

Walter Reed (1851–1902):

Army surgeon, born in Virginia. His investigations proved a certain kind of mosquito to be carrier of deadly yellow fever (1900). Hospital in Washington, D.C., named in his honor.

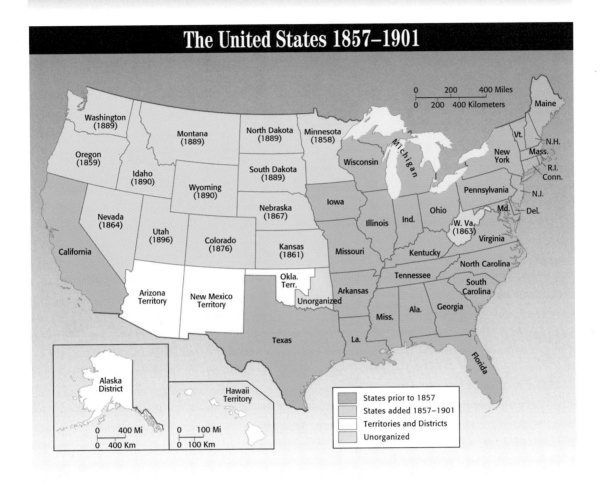

The United States 1857–1901

Washington (1889)

Oregon (1859)

Montana (1889)

North Dakota (1889)

Minnesota (1858)

Maine

Vt.

N.H.

Mass.

New York

R.I.
Conn.

Wisconsin

Michigan

Idaho (1890)

Wyoming (1890)

South Dakota (1889)

Pennsylvania

N.J.

Nevada (1864)

Utah (1896)

Colorado (1876)

Nebraska (1867)

Iowa

Illinois

Ind.

Ohio

Md.

Del.

W. Va. (1863)

Virginia

California

Kansas (1861)

Missouri

Kentucky

North Carolina

Arizona Territory

New Mexico Territory

Okla. Terr.

Unorganized

Arkansas

Tennessee

South Carolina

Miss.

Ala.

Georgia

Texas

La.

Florida

0   200   400 Miles
0   200   400 Kilometers

Alaska District

0   400 Mi
0   400 Km

Hawaii Territory

0   100 Mi
0   100 Km

States prior to 1857
States added 1857–1901
Territories and Districts
Unorganized

From 1857 to 1901, 13 states west of the Mississippi River were added to the United States, and West Virginia was carved out of the state of Virginia. In addition, Alaska was purchased, Hawaii was annexed, and Puerto Rico, Guam, and the Philippines became part of the nation.

15. James Buchanan (1857–1861)

Democratic party; age at inauguration, 65
Born: Mercersburg, Pennsylvania, April 23, 1791
Died: Lancaster, Pennsylvania, June 1, 1868
Education; occupation: Dickinson College; lawyer
Family: Bachelor
Important events during Buchanan's term:

    1857: Overland mail line established to California; economic depression;
          Dred Scott decision

    1858: Minnesota becomes 32nd state; Lincoln-Douglas debates

    1859: Oregon becomes 33rd state; John Brown's raid on Harpers Ferry, Virginia

    1860: Pony Express begins; South Carolina passes secession ordinance.

    1861: Kansas becomes 34th state; Southern Confederacy formed.

16. Abraham Lincoln (1861–1865)

Republican party; age at inauguration, 52
Born: Hodgenville, Kentucky, February 12, 1809
Died: Washington, D.C., April 15, 1865
Education; occupation: Self-educated; lawyer
Family: Mary Todd (married 1842);
  children: Robert, Edward, William, Thomas (Tad)
Important events during Lincoln's terms:

    1861: Civil War begins; Battle of First Manassas, Virginia

    1862: Battle of *Monitor* and *Merrimac*; Battles of Shiloh, Tennessee; Antietam,
          Maryland; Homestead Act

    1863: Emancipation Proclamation; West Virginia becomes 35th state;
          Battle of Gettysburg; Vicksburg surrenders; Gettysburg Address

    1864: Nevada becomes 36th state; Atlanta captured by Sherman.

    1865: Lee surrenders and Confederacy is defeated; Lincoln assassinated.

17. Andrew Johnson (1865–1869)

Democratic party; age at inauguration, 56

Born: Raleigh, North Carolina, December 29, 1808

Died: Carter's Station, Tennessee, July 31, 1875

Education; occupation: Self-educated, tailor

Family: Eliza McCardle (married 1827);

   children: Martha, Charles, Mary, Robert, Andrew

Important events during Johnson's term:

   1865: Jefferson Davis captured; Thirteenth Amendment ends slavery.

   1867: Reconstruction Acts; Nebraska becomes 37th state;
          Alaska purchased for $7.2 million.

   1868: Johnson impeached in House but not Senate;
          Fourteenth Amendment establishes equal rights.

18. Ulysses Simpson Grant (1869–1877)

Republican party; age at inauguration, 46

Born: Point Pleasant, Ohio, April 27, 1822

Died: Mt. McGregor, New York, July 23, 1885

Education; occupation: West Point; soldier

Family: Julia Dent (married 1848); children: Frederick, Ulysses, Ellen, Jesse

Important events during Grant's terms:

   1869: Transcontinental railroad service begins.

   1870: Fifteenth Amendment (voting rights) ratified.

   1871: Great Chicago Fire

   1876: Alexander Graham Bell successfully demonstrates the telephone;
          General G. A. Custer defeated at Little Big Horn, Montana;
          100th anniversary of signing of Declaration of Independence;
          Colorado becomes 38th state.

19. Rutherford Birchard Hayes (1877–1881)

Republican party; age at inauguration, 54

Born: Delaware, Ohio, October 4, 1822

Died: Fremont, Ohio, January 17, 1893

Education; occupation: Kenyon College, Harvard Law School; lawyer

Family: Lucy Ware Webb (married 1852);

   children: Birchard, Webb, Rutherford, Joseph, George, Fanny, Scott, Manning

Important events during Hayes's term:

    1877: End of Reconstruction

    1878: Edison gets phonograph patent.

    1879: Women permitted to practice law before Supreme Court;

           Edison invents electric light.

    1880: New York City population passes one million;

           Hayes first President to visit West Coast while in office.

20. James A. Garfield (1881)

Republican party; age at inauguration, 49

Born: Orange, Ohio, November 19, 1831

Died: Elberon, New Jersey, September 18, 1881

Education; occupation: Williams College; teacher

Family: Lucretia Rudolph (married 1858);

   children: Eliza, Harry, James, Mary, Irvin, Abram, Edward

Important events during Garfield's term:

    1881: Garfield shot by Charles J. Guiteau, second President to be assassinated.

21. Chester Alan Arthur (1881–1885)

Republican party; age at inauguration, 50

Born: Fairfield, Vermont, October 5, 1830

Died: New York City, November 18, 1886

Education; occupation: Union College; lawyer

Family: Ellen Lewis Herndon (married 1859);

   children: William, Chester Jr., Ellen

Important events during Arthur's term:

    1883: Standard time adopted.

    1885: Washington Monument dedicated.

22, 24. Grover Cleveland (1885–1889; 1893–1897)

Democratic party; age at first inauguration, 47

Born: Caldwell, New Jersey, March 18, 1837

Died: Princeton, New Jersey, June 24, 1908

Education; occupation: Public schools; lawyer

Family: Frances Folsom (married 1886);

   children: Ruth, Esther, Marion, Richard, Francis

Important events during Cleveland's terms:

    1886: Presidential Succession Act approved; Statue of Liberty dedicated.

    1893: Severe depression

    1894: Federal troops quell Pullman strike.

    1896: Utah becomes 45th state.

23. Benjamin Harrison (1889–1893)

Republican party; age at inauguration, 55

Born: North Bend, Ohio, August 20, 1833

Died: Indianapolis, Indiana, March 13, 1901

Education; occupation: Miami University of Ohio; lawyer

Family: (1) Caroline Scott (married 1853);
    children: Russell, Mary. (2) Mary Dimmick (married 1896);
    children: Elizabeth

Important events during Harrison's term:

    1889: Johnstown, Pennsylvania, flood; North Dakota becomes 39th state;
        South Dakota becomes 40th state; Montana becomes 41st state;
        Washington becomes 42nd state.

    1890: Sherman Antitrust Law; Idaho becomes 43rd state;
        Wyoming becomes 44th state; McKinley Tariff Act

25. William McKinley (1897–1901)

Republican party; age at inauguration, 54

Born: Niles, Ohio, January 29, 1843

Died: Buffalo, New York, September 14, 1901

Education; occupation: Allegheny College; lawyer

Family: Ida Saxton (married 1871); children: Katherine, Ida

Important events during McKinley's term:

    1898: Battleship *Maine* blown up in Havana, Cuba; U.S. declares war on Spain;
        U.S. annexes Hawaiian Islands; Treaty of Paris ends Spanish-American
        War; Puerto Rico, Guam, Philippines become part of U.S.

    1901: McKinley becomes third President assassinated.

Glossary

abolitionist A social reformer who spoke out against slavery and worked to end the practice.

anarchist One who does not believe in any form of governmental authority and who wants to overthrow the existing government by force.

arbitration The process of settling differences peacefully between or among opposing parties.

assassination The act of murder by sudden or secret attack, generally used when involving politically important figure.

bombardment Persistent attack, especially with artillery or bombers, as bombardment of Fort Sumter to begin Civil War.

depression In economics, a period of low activity, usually marked by high unemployment.

espionage The use of spies to obtain information about a foreign country.

fanatic Intense, sometimes frenzied, devotion to a cause, often political or religious, generally used today regarding sports, e.g., a football fanatic.

impeach To charge a public official with an illegal act while in office.

mudslinging The act of using offensive, usually personal, attacks against a political opponent.

plantation system A cultivated system of agriculture, usually involving some kind of resident labor.

platform The principles and plans of a political party or candidate.

secession Formal withdrawal from an organization or nation.

spoils system The practice of awarding government appointments based on contributions to the victor's election rather than merit; frowned upon today but still in use.

tariff Government-imposed charges on imported, or sometimes exported, goods

Further Reading

Altman, Linda J. *The Pullman Strike of Eighteen Ninety-Four: Turning Point for American Labor*. Millbrook, 1994

Brown, Fern G. *James A. Garfield: Twentieth President of the United States*. Garrett, 1990

Carter, Alden R. *Spanish-American War: Imperial Ambitions*. Franklin Watts, 1992

Collins, David R. *Grover Cleveland: Twenty-Second and Twenty-Fourth President of the United States*. Garrett, 1990

_____. *William McKinley: Twenty-Fifth President of the United States*. Garrett, 1990

Colman, Penny. *Strike! The Bitter Struggle of American Workers from Colonial Times to the Present*. Millbrook, 1995

Dash, Joan. *We Shall Not Be Moved: The Women's Factory Strike of 1909*. Scholastic, 1996

Durwood, Thomas A. *Andrew Johnson: Rebuilding the Union*. Silver Burdett, 1990

Falkof, Lucille. *Ulysses S. Grant: Eighteenth President of the United States*. Garrett, 1988

Feinberg, Barbara S. *American Political Scandals Past and Present*. Franklin Watts, 1992

Gay, Kathlyn. *Civil War*. Holt, 1995

Herb, Angela M. *Beyond the Mississippi: Early Western Expansion of the United States*. Lodestar, 1996

Lindop, Edmund. *Assassinations that Shook America*. Franklin Watts, 1992

_____. *Presidents vs. Congress: Conflict and Compromise*. Franklin Watts, 1994

McNeer, May. *America's Abraham Lincoln*. Marshall Cavendish, 1991

Meltzer, Milton. *Bread and Roses: The Struggle of American Labor, 1865-1915*. Facts on File, 1990

Mettger, Zak. *Reconstruction: America After the Civil War*. Dutton, 1994

Morin, Isobel V. *Impeaching the President*. Millbrook, 1996

O'Brian, Steven. *Ulysses S. Grant*. Chelsea House, 1991

Potter, Robert R. *John Brown: Militant Abolitionist*. Raintree Steck-Vaughn, 1995

Robbins, Neal E. *Rutherford B. Hayes: Nineteenth President of the United States*. Garrett, 1989

Smith, John David. *Black Voices from Reconstruction, 1865-1877*. Millbrook, 1996

Stevens, Rita. *Andrew Johnson: Seventeenth President of the United States*. Garrett, 1989

_____. *Benjamin Harrison: Twenty-Third President of the United States*. Garrett, 1989

Young, Robert. *Emancipation Proclamation: Why Lincoln Really Freed the Slaves*. Macmillan, 1994

Index